■SCHOLASTIC

2

Morning Jumpstarts: Reading

100 Independent Practice Pages to Build Essential Skills

Marcia Miller & Martin Lee

New York · Toronto · London · Auckland · Sydney
Mexico City · New Delhi · Hong Kong · Buenos Aires

Teaching *Resources*

Scholastic Inc. grants teachers permission to photocopy the reproducible pages from this book for classroom use. No other part of this publication may be reproduced in whole or in part, or stored in a retrieval system, or transmitted in any form or by any means, electronic, mechanical, photocopying, recording, or otherwise, without written permission of the publisher. For information regarding permission, write to Scholastic Inc., 557 Broadway, New York, NY 10012.

Cover design by Scott Davis

Interior design by Sydney Wright

Interior illustrations by Teresa Anderko, Maxie Chambliss, Rusty Fletcher, Mike Gordon, James Graham Hale, Anne Kennedy, Sydney Wright, and Bari Weissman; © 2013 by Scholastic Inc.

Image credits: page 24 © stockcreations/Shutterstock; page 54 © Elias H. Debbas II/Shutterstock; page 72 © Matthew Cole/Shutterstock; page 80 © isaxar/Shutterstock; page 104 © Clouds Hill Imaging Ltd./Corbis

ISBN: 978-0-545-46421-5

Copyright © 2013 by Scholastic Inc.

All rights reserved.
Printed in the U.S.A.
Published by Scholastic Inc.

1 2 3 4 5 6 7 8 9 10   40   20 19 18 17 16 15 14 13

Contents

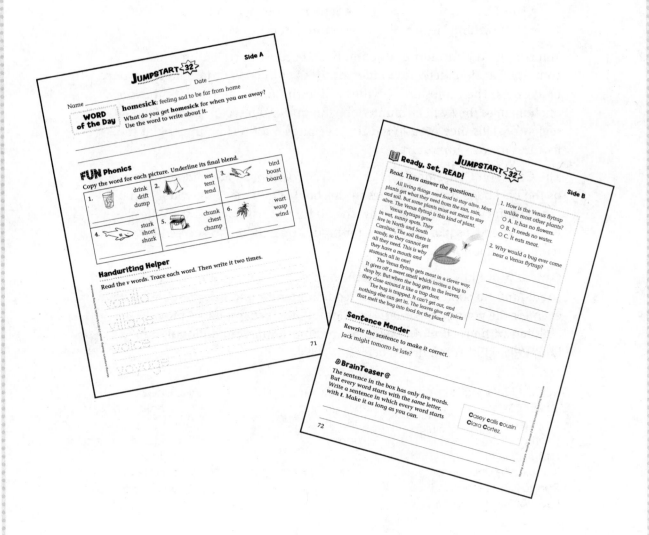

Introduction

In your busy classroom, you know how vital it is to energize children for the tasks of the day. That's why *Morning Jumpstarts: Reading, Grade 2* is the perfect tool for you.

The activities in this book provide brief and focused individual practice on grade-level skills children are expected to master. Each Jumpstart is a two-page collection of six activities designed to review and reinforce a range of reading and writing skills children will build throughout the year. The consistent format helps children work independently and with confidence. Each Jumpstart includes these features:

- Word of the Day
- Fun Phonics
- Handwriting Helper
- Ready, Set, Read!
- Sentence Mender
- Brainteaser

You can use a Jumpstart in its entirety or, because each feature is self-contained, assign sections at different times of the day or to different groups of learners. The Jumpstart activities will familiarize children with the kinds of challenges they will encounter on standardized tests, and provide a review of skills they need to master. (See page 6 for a close-up look at the features in each Jumpstart.)

The Common Core State Standards (CCSS) for English Language Arts serve as the backbone of the activities in this book. On pages 7–8, you'll find a correlation chart that details how the 50 Jumpstarts dovetail with the widely accepted set of guidelines for preparing children to succeed in reading and language arts.

Generally, we have kept in mind the four CCSS "anchor standards" that should inform solid instruction in reading literary and informational texts, even for the youngest learners. In addition, the activity pages provide children with practice in developing and mastering foundational and language skills, summarized below.

ANCHOR STANDARDS
FOR READING
- Key Ideas and Details
- Craft and Structure
- Integration of Knowledge and Ideas
- Range of Reading and Level of Text Complexity

FOUNDATIONAL SKILLS
- Phonics and Word Recognition
- Fluency

LANGUAGE
- Conventions of Standard English
- Knowledge of Language
- Vocabulary Acquisition and Use

Morning Jumpstarts: Reading, Grade 2 © 2013 Scholastic Teaching Resources

How to Use This Book

Morning Jumpstarts: Reading, Grade 2 can be used in many ways—and not just in the morning! You know your students best, so feel free to pick and choose among the activities, and incorporate those you see fit. You can make double-sided copies, or print one side at a time and staple the pages together.

We suggest the following times to present Jumpstarts:

- At the start of the school day, as a way to help children settle into the day's routines.
- Before lunch, as children ready themselves for their midday break.
- After lunch, as a calming transition into the afternoon's plans.
- Toward the end of the day, before children gather their belongings to go home, or for homework.

In general, the Jumpstarts progress in difficulty level and build on skills covered in previous sheets. Preview each one before you assign it, to ensure that the children in your class have the skills needed to complete them. Keep in mind, however, that you may opt for some children to skip sections, as appropriate, or complete them together at a later time as part of a small-group or whole-class lesson.

Undoubtedly, children will complete their Jumpstart activity pages at different rates. We suggest that you set up a "what to do when I'm done" plan to give children who need more time a chance to finish without interruption. For example, you might encourage children to complete another Jumpstart. They might also choose to read silently, practice handwriting, journal, or engage in other kinds of writing.

An answer key begins on page 109. You might want to review answers with the whole class. This approach provides opportunities for discussion, comparison, extension, reinforcement, and correlation to other skills and lessons in your current plans. Your observations can direct the kinds of review or reinforcement you may want to add to your lessons. Alternatively, you may find that having children discuss activity solutions and strategies in small groups is another effective approach.

When you introduce the first Jumpstart, walk through its features with your class to provide an overview before you assign it and to make sure children understand the directions. Help children see that the activities in each section focus on different kinds of skills, and let them know that the same sections will repeat throughout each Jumpstart, always in the same order and position. You might want to work through the first few Jumpstarts as a group until children are comfortable with the routine and ready to work independently.

You know best how to assign the work to the children in your class. You might, for instance, stretch a Jumpstart over two days, assigning Side A on the first day and Side B on the second. Although the activities on different Jumpstarts vary in difficulty and in time needed, we anticipate that once children are familiar with the routine, most will be able to complete both sides of a Jumpstart in anywhere from 10 to 20 minutes.

A Look Inside

Each two-page Jumpstart includes the following skill-building features.

Word of the Day The first feature on Side A builds vocabulary. Children read a grade-appropriate word and its definition. A brief writing task asks them to use the new word to demonstrate understanding of its proper usage.

Fun Phonics Every Side A presents a grade-appropriate word-study feature that focuses on a key phonics or word-study topic. For more capable learners, this activity may provide review. Students who need more support may need guidance or hints to help them succeed.

Handwriting Helper This feature rounds out Side A by offering students a chance to practice manuscript handwriting. The words and phrases encompass practice of both lower- and uppercase letters.

Ready, Set, Read! Every Side B begins with a brief reading passage, followed by two or more text-based questions. Passages include fiction and nonfiction, prose and poetry, folktales, serious and humorous writing, realistic and fantastical settings. Dig deeper into any passage to inspire discussion, questions, and extension.

Tell children to first read the passage and then answer the questions. Show them how to fill in the circles for multiple-choice questions. For questions that require children to write, encourage them to use another sheet of paper, if needed.

Sentence Mender The second Side B feature addresses grade-appropriate conventions of standard English, especially spelling, capitalization, punctuation, and grammar. Children will see a sentence with errors. Their task is to rewrite the sentence correctly. A sample answer is given in the Answer Key, but it is quite possible that children may devise alternate corrections. Link this task to the revising and proofreading steps of the writing process.

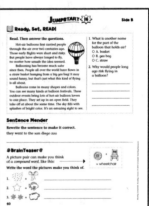

Brainteaser Side B always ends with some form of an entertaining word or language challenge: a puzzle, code, riddle, or other engaging task designed to stretch the mind. While some children may find this section particularly challenging, others will relish teasing out tricky solutions. This feature provides another chance for group work or discussion. It may prove useful to have pairs of children tackle these together. And, when appropriate, invite children to create their own challenges, using ideas sparked by these exercises. Feel free to create your own variations of any brainteasers your class enjoys.

Morning Jumpstarts: Reading, Grade 2 © 2013 Scholastic Teaching Resources

Connections to the Common Core State Standards

As shown in the chart below and on page 8, the activities in this book will help you meet your specific state reading and language arts standards as well as those outlined in the CCSS. These materials address the following standards for students in grade 2. For details on these standards, visit the CCSS Web site: **www.corestandards.org/the-standards/**.

JS	Reading: Literature								Reading: Informational Text									Reading: Foundational Skills			Language					
	2.RL.1	2.RL.2	2.RL.3	2.RL.4	2.RL.5	2.RL.6	2.RL.7	2.RL.10	2.RI.1	2.RI.2	2.RI.3	2.RI.4	2.RI.5	2.RI.6	2.RI.7	2.RI.8	2.RI.10	2.RF.3	2.RF.4		2.L.1	2.L.2	2.L.3	2.L.4	2.L.5	2.L.6
1									•	•	•	•		•	•	•	•	•	•		•	•	•	•		•
2	•	•	•	•	•	•	•	•										•	•		•	•	•	•	•	•
3									•	•	•	•	•	•	•	•	•	•	•		•	•	•	•	•	•
4									•	•	•	•	•			•	•	•	•		•	•	•	•	•	•
5	•	•	•	•		•	•	•										•	•		•	•	•	•		•
6	•	•	•	•		•	•	•										•	•		•	•	•	•		•
7									•	•		•		•	•	•	•	•	•		•	•	•	•	•	•
8									•	•	•	•		•	•	•	•	•	•		•	•	•	•		•
9									•	•	•		•	•	•	•	•	•	•		•	•	•	•	•	•
10									•	•	•	•				•	•	•	•		•	•	•	•		•
11	•	•	•	•			•	•										•	•		•	•	•	•		•
12									•	•		•	•					•	•		•	•	•	•	•	•
13	•	•		•	•	•	•	•										•	•		•	•	•	•	•	•
14	•	•	•		•	•	•	•										•	•		•	•	•	•	•	•
15	•	•	•		•	•	•											•	•		•	•	•	•	•	•
16									•	•	•			•	•			•	•		•	•	•	•	•	•
17	•	•	•		•		•	•										•	•		•	•	•	•	•	•
18	•		•				•	•										•	•		•	•	•	•	•	•
19									•	•	•		•	•	•	•	•	•	•		•	•	•	•	•	•
20									•	•	•	•		•	•	•	•	•	•		•	•	•	•	•	•
21	•	•	•	•		•	•	•										•	•		•	•	•	•	•	•
22	•	•	•	•	•	•	•	•										•	•		•	•	•	•	•	•
23	•	•	•			•	•	•										•	•		•	•	•	•	•	•
24	•	•	•		•		•	•										•	•		•	•		•	•	•
25	•			•			•	•										•	•		•	•		•		•

Connections to the Common Core State Standards

JS	2.RL.1	2.RL.2	2.RL.3	2.RL.4	2.RL.5	2.RL.6	2.RL.7	2.RL.10	2.RI.1	2.RI.2	2.RI.3	2.RI.4	2.RI.5	2.RI.6	2.RI.7	2.RI.8	2.RI.10	2.RF.3	2.RF.4	2.L.1	2.L.2	2.L.3	2.L.4	2.L.5	2.L.6
	Reading: Literature								Reading: Informational Text									Reading: Foundational Skills		Language					
26	•		•	•	•	•	•	•										•	•	•	•	•	•		•
27	•	•	•				•	•										•	•	•	•	•	•	•	•
28									•	•	•	•		•	•	•	•	•	•	•	•	•	•		•
29	•	•	•			•	•	•										•	•	•	•	•	•		•
30	•	•	•	•	•	•		•										•	•	•	•	•	•		•
31	•	•	•	•	•	•	•	•										•	•	•	•	•			•
32									•	•	•	•		•	•	•	•	•	•	•	•	•	•		•
33	•	•	•	•			•	•										•	•	•	•	•	•		•
34									•	•	•	•			•	•	•	•	•	•	•		•		•
35	•	•	•	•		•	•	•										•	•	•	•	•	•		•
36									•	•	•	•		•	•	•	•	•	•	•	•	•	•		•
37	•	•		•	•	•		•										•	•	•	•	•	•		•
38									•	•		•			•	•	•	•	•	•	•	•	•		•
39									•	•	•	•		•	•	•	•	•	•	•	•	•	•		•
40	•	•	•	•		•	•	•										•	•	•	•	•	•		•
41									•	•	•	•			•	•	•	•	•	•	•	•	•		•
42									•	•	•	•						•	•	•	•	•	•		•
43	•	•	•				•	•											•	•	•	•	•		•
44	•	•	•		•		•	•											•	•	•	•	•		•
45	•	•	•	•	•														•	•	•	•	•		•
46									•	•	•	•	•			•	•	•	•	•	•	•	•		•
47									•	•	•	•				•		•	•	•	•	•	•		•
48									•	•	•	•			•	•		•	•	•	•	•	•	•	•
49	•	•	•	•	•	•		•										•	•	•	•	•	•		•
50									•	•		•			•		•	•		•		•	•		•

8

Name _John_   Date _May 6th, 2017_

Morning Jumpstarts: Reading, Grade 2 © 2013 Scholastic Teaching Resources

WORD of the Day

pair: two things that match or go together

Use the word **pair** to write about something that comes in twos.

Do you need a pair of scissors?

FUN Phonics

Name each picture. Write the letter that stands for the **beginning** sound.

1.  _B_
2.  _H_
3.  _D_
4. 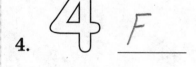 _F_
5. 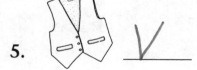 _V_
6.  _m_

Handwriting Helper

Read the *people* words. Trace each word. Then write it two times.

boy   boy   boy

girl   girl   girl

man   man   man

woman   woman   woman

📖 Ready, Set, READ!

Read. Then answer the questions.

"Once in a blue moon" is an old saying. It is not about the color of the moon. It is a way to say that an event is rare.

Each month has one full moon. It may appear any time in the month. But every few years, a month has two full moons. That second full moon in the same month is the blue moon.

1. What does "once in a blue moon" mean?

   ● A. once a month   ○ B. twice a week   ○ C. not very often

2. Can there ever be a blue moon on May 1? Explain.

   _____

   _____

Sentence Mender

Rewrite the sentence to make it correct.

Dad a shopping list.

Dad has a sopping list

☺ BrainTeaser ☺

Unscramble each color word. Write it correctly in the spaces. The letters in the boxes will spell another color word. Write the new word on the line below.

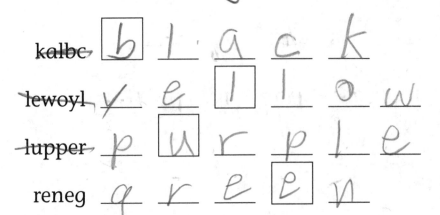

kalbc — b l a c k

lewoyl — y e l l o w

lupper — p u r p l e

reneg — g r e e n

The color word is *blue*.

Morning Jumpstarts: Reading, Grade 2 © 2013 Scholastic Teaching Resources

Name _John_ Date _May 7, 2017_

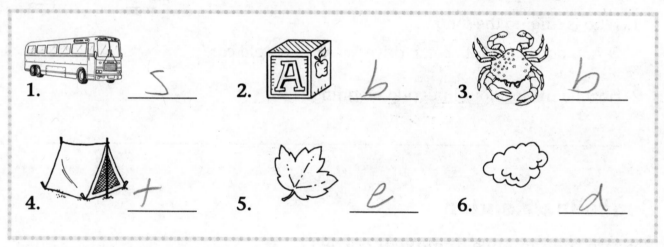

WORD of the Day

busy: working on things; having a lot to do

Use the word **busy** to write about what you do on a rainy day.

I was busy doing my homework that I did not kown it was raining

FUN Phonics

Name each picture. Write the letter that stands for the **ending** sound.

1. _s_   2. _b_   3. _b_

4. _t_   5. _e_   6. _d_

Handwriting Helper

Read the *people* words. Trace each word. Then write it two times.

person person person

human human human

child child child

children children children

Morning Jumpstarts: Reading, Grade 2 © 2013 Scholastic Teaching Resources

 ## Ready, Set, READ!

Read. Then answer the questions.

The Car Song *Author Unknown*

I'm a little hunk of tin.
Nobody knows the shape I'm in.
Got four wheels and a steering bar.
I'm an old-time worn-out car.

Honk rattle honk rattle crash beep beep!
Honk rattle honk rattle crash beep beep!
Honk rattle honk rattle crash beep beep!
Funky junky worn-out car!

1. Who is singing the song?

   ○ A. a doctor   ○ B. a cab driver   ◉ C. an old car

2. How do the last four lines add meaning?

   _____

Sentence Mender

Rewrite the sentence to make it correct.

jason red the whole book.

Jason read the whole book.

☻ BrainTeaser ☻

Unscramble each number word.
Write it correctly in the spaces.
The letters in the boxes will
spell another number word.
Write the new word on the
line below.

urof   f o u r

enni   n i n e

venes   s e v e n

roze   z e r o

The number word is _five_.

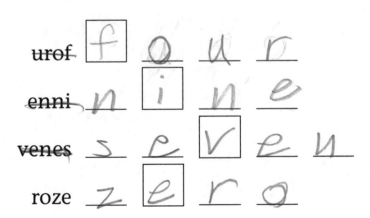

Morning Jumpstarts: Reading, Grade 2 © 2013 Scholastic Teaching Resources

Name ___John___   Date ___May 9th, 2017___

Morning Jumpstarts: Reading, Grade 2 © 2013 Scholastic Teaching Resources

WORD of the Day

boast: to talk too highly about yourself; brag

Use the word **boast** to describe how you feel when a friend brags to you.

_____

_____

FUN Phonics

Name each picture. Write the letter that stands for the **middle** sound.

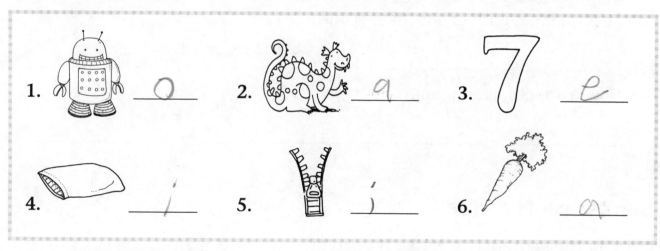

1. ___o___   2. ___a___   3. ___e___

4. ___i___   5. ___i___   6. ___a___

Handwriting Helper

Read the words about writing. Trace each word. Then write it two times.

pencil pencil pencil

space space space

line line line

loop loop loop

Ready, Set, READ!

Read. Then answer the questions.

Your teeth are alive! They began to form before you were born. They will keep growing until you are an adult.

Every tooth has two main parts: the crown and the root.

- The **crown** is the top of the tooth. It's the white part you see above the gum line.
- The **root** is the rest of your tooth. It is below the gum line. You can't see it, but the root is twice as long as the crown. It holds the tooth in place, feeds the tooth, and has nerves that sense pain.

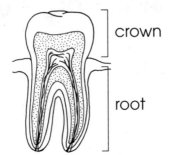

1. The two main parts of a tooth are called

   the ___crown___ and the ___root___.

2. How is a tooth like a plant?

   _____

Sentence Mender

Rewrite the sentence to make it correct.

Did You rite this poem

Did you write this poem

⑨ BrainTeaser ⑥

Unscramble each month name. Write it correctly in the spaces. The letters in the boxes will spell another calendar word. Write the new word on the line below.

yam   M a y

unje   J u n e

lipar   A p r i l

charm   m a r c h

The calendar word is ___year___.

Morning Jumpstarts: Reading, Grade 2 © 2013 Scholastic Teaching Resources

Name _____ Date _____

Morning Jumpstarts: Reading, Grade 2 © 2013 Scholastic Teaching Resources

WORD of the Day

dune: a hill of sand piled up by wind

Use the word **dune** to tell where you would probably see one.

_____

_____

FUN Phonics

Where's the **T** in each word? Name each picture. Listen for its **T** sound. Write **B** for *beginning*, **M** for *middle*, or **E** for *end*.

1.  _____

2.  _____

3.  _____

4.  _____

5. _____

6.  _____

Handwriting Helper

Read the words about the human body. Trace each word. Then write it two times.

ankle

chest

elbow

wrist

Ready, Set, READ!

Read. Then answer the questions.

 FROST SCHOOL FALL FAIR
Saturday, September 30
10 AM to 4 PM

Our great Fall Fair is back! You will find fun events for kids of all ages. Play with your friends and teachers. Bring the whole family. Stay for a little while. Or stay all day. This year you can enjoy these events:

- Craft City
- Book Booth
- Contests and Rides
- Food and Drinks
- Music and Dancing
- Petting Zoo
- Science Lab
- Sports and Games

1. On what day is the fair?
   - ○ A. Fall
   - ○ B. Friday
   - ○ C. Saturday

2. Where could you hold a lamb?

   _____

   _____

3. Where could you make a puppet?

   _____

   _____

Sentence Mender

Rewrite the sentence to make it correct.

My bedtime is ate o'clock

_____

⟲ BrainTeaser ⟳

Write two other words whose letters fit the same shape.

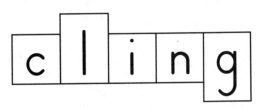

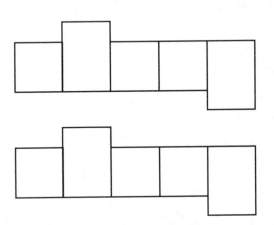

Morning Jumpstarts: Reading, Grade 2 © 2013 Scholastic Teaching Resources

Name _____ Date _____

Morning Jumpstarts: Reading, Grade 2 © 2013 Scholastic Teaching Resources

WORD of the Day

glum: feeling sad, low, or gloomy

Use the word **glum** to write about what can make you feel that way.

_____

_____

FUN Phonics

Write **m**, **n**, or **r** to complete each word.

1. lu _____ p

2. sc _____ ap

3. fi _____ d

4. fil _____

5. _____ oise

6. _____ arble

7. drai _____

8. _____ attle

9. neve _____

Handwriting Helper

Read the words about books. Trace each word. Then write it two times.

page

word

cover

chapter

Ready, Set, READ!

Read. Then answer the questions.

Kita had a new outfit, backpack, and fresh pencils. She knew her new address and phone number. The bus stop was near her house. She had seen the new school when her mom signed her up. But this was her first real school day. She was worried. Who would be in her class? Would she like the teacher? Would she fit in?

A yellow bus pulled up and opened its door. Kita took a breath and climbed on. She smiled at the driver. But the driver just barked, "Find a seat and buckle up." Kita's smile faded. She sat down, tried not to cry, and looked out the window.

1. What makes this trip to school different for Kita?

_____

2. What does it mean that the driver *barked*?

_____

Sentence Mender

Rewrite the sentence to make it correct.

Please dont say those mean word

_____

☺ BrainTeaser ☺

Write two other words whose letters fit the same shape.

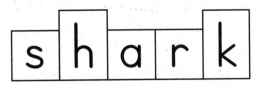

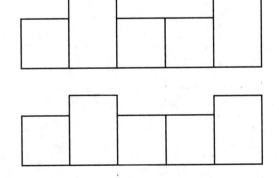

Morning Jumpstarts: Reading, Grade 2 © 2013 Scholastic Teaching Resources

Name _____ Date _____

WORD of the Day

grasp: to understand

Use the word **grasp** to write about a hard idea you want to understand.

_____

_____

FUN Phonics

Letter Bank

a e i o u

Fill in the missing vowels. Use the letter bank.
Read the words.

1.  be ____ lt   2. 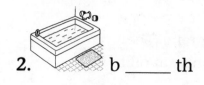 b ____ th   3. 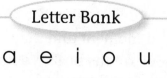 b ____ ll

4.  b ____ ll   5.  b ____ ll   6.  b ____ ll

Handwriting Helper

Read the words about costumes. Trace each word. Then write it two times.

wig _____

mask _____

cape _____

crown _____

📖 Ready, Set, READ!

Read. Then answer the questions.

The Crow and the Dog *A Tagalog Folktale*

One day a crow saw some fresh meat drying in the sun. The crow swooped down and snatched a piece of meat. He flew into a nearby tree, where he began to eat.

On the ground below lay a hungry dog who saw what the crow did. He thought for a moment and then called up, "O great crow! Of all the birds, you are by far the best and brightest!"

The crow laughed with joy at the dog's kind words. But the moment the crow opened its beak, the meat fell to the ground. The clever dog grabbed the meat and ran off to its den with it.

So children, beware. Kind words can also be used to trick you.

1. Why was the fresh meat outside?
   - ○ A. because it was winter
   - ○ B. to dry in the sun
   - ○ C. to feed the wild birds

2. What made the crow drop the meat?
   - ○ A. He got frightened.
   - ○ B. He was done eating.
   - ○ C. The dog made him feel good.

Sentence Mender

Rewrite the sentence to make it correct.

My sister katy didint shut door.

_____

☺ BrainTeaser ☺

How many different words can you spell with letters from the word **strawberry**? Every word must have at least three letters. List them here.

_____

_____

_____

Morning Jumpstarts: Reading, Grade 2 © 2013 Scholastic Teaching Resources

Name _____ Date _____

WORD of the Day	**chore**: a small job you have to do

Use the word **chore** to describe a small job you do at school or at home.

_____

_____

FUN Phonics

Write two different words for each short-*a* word family.
One is done for you.

-ack	-ap	-ank	-ash	-at
black				

Handwriting Helper

Read the *comparing* words. Trace each word. Then write it two times.

same _____

like _____

equal _____

match _____

Ready, Set, READ!

Read. Then answer the questions.

Hi Krista,

    I love it in Virginia. We've been to the beach near Gram's house every day so far. After we swim, we bring back shells for Gram's porch. At night, we cook out in her yard and eat in the gazebo (guh-ZEE-bo). A gazebo is a little screened-in house out in the garden. It keeps the bugs out. I read there in the mornings.

    Tomorrow, we visit a horse farm. Gramps has a friend who works there. He'll give us a tour of the stables and the training ring. We might ride with him in the tractor to take hay to the field horses. I can't wait! I wish you were here, too.

    See you in August.

Your friend,
Eva

1. What time of year did Eva write the postcard?
   - ○ A. winter
   - ○ B. summer
   - ○ C. can't tell

2. Describe a *gazebo* in your own words.

   _____

   _____

   _____

   _____

   _____

   _____

Sentence Mender

Rewrite the sentence to make it correct.

Mike gave we a ride in her new car.

_____

◉ BrainTeaser ◉

An *anagram* is a new word you make with all the letters of another word. **Act** is an anagram for **cat**.

Make an anagram for each word.

1. ram ⟺ _____

2. tap ⟺ _____

3. grin ⟺ _____

4. pots ⟺ _____

Morning Jumpstarts: Reading, Grade 2 © 2013 Scholastic Teaching Resources

Name _____ Date _____

| WORD of the Day | **polite**: well-behaved and thoughtful to others |

Use the word **polite** to write about a thoughtful thing you might do at a store.

_____

_____

FUN Phonics

Write two different words for each short-*e* word family.
One is done for you.

-ell	-est	-eck	-ent	-ess
well				

Handwriting Helper

Read the *calendar* words. Trace each word. Then write it.

week _____

Sunday _____

Monday _____

Tuesday _____

Ready, Set, READ!

Read. Then answer the questions.

You use money made of metal coins and paper bills. But money wasn't always made of metal and paper. People of the past used all kinds of things as money. They used any items that others wanted. Feathers, stones, shells, and salt were all used as money at one time.

Item	Cocoa Beans
tomato	1
egg	3
rabbit	30
white cape	65

You may know that chocolate comes from the cocoa plant. Cocoa trees grew in many parts of Mexico. Cocoa was once used only by rich kings. They made it into a drink. And they used it as money.

People traded cocoa for things they needed. The table shows what some things cost in cocoa beans.

1. How many cocoa beans would two eggs cost?

_____

2. Which was *not* used as money?

   ○ A. salt   ○ B. stones   ○ C. hair

Sentence Mender

Rewrite the sentence to make it correct.

your class was go to the park

_____

☺ BrainTeaser ☺

An *anagram* is a new word you make with all the letters of another word. **Act** is an anagram for **cat**.

Make an anagram for each word.

1. bowl ⇔ _____   3. stew ⇔ _____

2. plum ⇔ _____   4. east ⇔ _____

Morning Jumpstarts: Reading, Grade 2 © 2013 Scholastic Teaching Resources

Name _____ Date _____

WORD of the Day

glide: to move along in a smooth, easy way

Use the word **glide** to describe how it feels to slide across a slippery floor.

_____

_____

FUN Phonics

Write two different words for each short-*i* word family.
One is done for you.

-ick	-ill	-ing	-ink	-itch
brick				

Handwriting Helper

Read the words for the days of the week.
Trace each word. Then write it.

Wednesday _____

Thursday _____

Friday _____

Saturday _____

📖 Ready, Set, READ!

Read. Then answer the questions.

What You Need
- plastic wrap
- pinecone
- string
- spoon
- peanut butter
- birdseed

Steps

1. Spread out some plastic wrap. Lay the pinecone in the middle of it.

2. Tie a string loop around the top of the pinecone.

3. Spread peanut butter on the pinecone.

4. Roll the pinecone in birdseed. Then hang it outside for the birds.

1. How many things do you need to get before you start?

  ○ A. 4   ○ B. 6   ○ C. 10

2. What is the string for?

_____

3. What is the spoon for? _____

Sentence Mender

Rewrite the sentence to make it correct.

the Teacher sed to shut ar eyes.

_____

☺ BrainTeaser ☺

Hink Pinks are word pairs that rhyme.
They answer riddles. Here's a Hink Pink: ⟶

What is a large kitten?
fat cat

Solve these Hink Pink riddles. Fill in the missing word for each.

1. What is a large stick? _____ **twig**

2. What is a chicken's cage? _____ **pen**

3. What is a cap you sat on? _____ **hat**

Morning Jumpstarts: Reading, Grade 2 © 2013 Scholastic Teaching Resources

Name _____ Date _____

○△○△○△○△○△○△○△○△○△○△
WORD of the Day
▽○▽○▽○▽○▽○▽○▽○▽○▽○▽○

distract: to draw attention away; bother, confuse

Use the word **distract** to describe sounds that bother you.

_____

_____

FUN Phonics

Write two different words for each short-*o* word family.
One is done for you.

-ock	-op	-ob	-og	-ox
block				

Handwriting Helper

Read the *time* words. Trace each word. Then write it two times.

time _____

clock _____

hour _____

minute _____

Ready, Set, READ!

Read. Then answer the questions.

Kermit the frog was born in 1955. His father was Jim Henson. Henson made Kermit for a puppet show called *Sam and Friends*. It was on TV for six years. Kermit was not a star. He wasn't even a frog yet. Henson said he looked more like a lizard.

Over the next few years, Kermit began to look more like a frog. In 1969, he tried out for a new show called *Sesame Street*. He got the part and became a full frog. He worked with other Muppets to sing, dance, talk, and tell jokes to children all over the world.

Kermit got his big break in 1976 as host of *The Muppet Show*. He went on to make movies, write books, and record albums.

1. What new fact did you learn from this passage?

_____

_____

_____

_____

_____

2. How old was Kermit when he began to host *The Muppet Show*?

_____

Sentence Mender

Rewrite the sentence to make it correct.

yesterDay we have pizza for Lunch.

๑ BrainTeaser ๑

Climb the word ladder to change **bat** into **pig**. Change one letter at a time. Write the *new* word on each step.

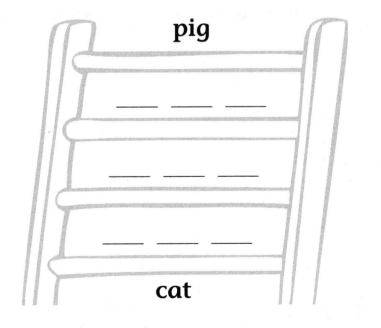

pig

cat

Morning Jumpstarts: Reading, Grade 2 © 2013 Scholastic Teaching Resources

Name _____ Date _____

WORD of the Day

hollow: empty inside; with space in the center

Use the word **hollow** to describe an object that is fun to play with.

_____

_____

FUN Phonics

Write two different words for each short-*u* word family.
One is done for you.

-uck	-ug	-ump	-unk	-ush
duck				

Handwriting Helper

Read the *calendar* words. Trace each word. Then write it two times.

day

week

month

year

Ready, Set, READ!

Read. Then answer the questions.

Issun-bōshi   *A Japanese Folktale*

In Japan, a very old couple longed for a child. "Oh please," they prayed, "give us a child, no matter how small." After some time, the old woman had a baby son. The couple was happy, though the baby was as small as a peanut! They named the boy Issun-bōshi. This name means Inch Son.

Issun-bōshi's parents loved him deeply. They cared for him with kindness. He grew into a bright and honest young man. But his body stayed as tiny as ever.

Issun-bōshi decided to travel the world to seek his fate. His parents wept to see him go, but they trusted him to act wisely. They gave him three gifts: a sewing needle as a sword, a rice bowl as a boat, and chopsticks as oars.

1. Why didn't the old couple mind that Issun-bōshi was so tiny?

_____

_____

_____

_____

_____

2. Which word does *not* tell about Issun-bōshi as a young man?
   - ○ A. bright
   - ○ B. tall
   - ○ C. honest

Sentence Mender

Rewrite the sentence to make it correct.

the wind blue down a tree near me house.

_____

☺ BrainTeaser ☺

Climb the word ladder to change **tick** into **tock**. Change one letter at a time. Write the *new* word on each step.

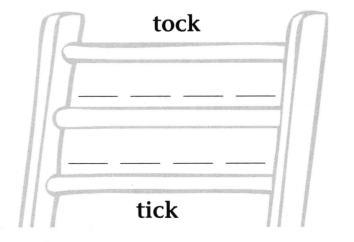

tock

tick

Morning Jumpstarts: Reading, Grade 2 © 2013 Scholastic Teaching Resources

Name _____ Date _____

☆☆☆☆☆☆☆☆☆☆☆☆☆☆☆

WORD of the Day

claim: to say something you believe is true

Use the word **claim** to explain an idea of your own.

_____

_____

FUN Phonics

Write the word name for each picture.

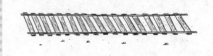

1. _____

2. _____

3. _____

4. _____

5. _____

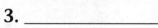

6. _____

Handwriting Helper

Read the *time* words. Trace each word. Then write it two times.

morning

noon

evening

night

Ready, Set, READ!

Read. Then answer the questions.

Hey Dad,

　　We are having a Job Fair on October 8. Kids are asking parents to come tell about their jobs. I think your job is cool, so I hope you can take part. You don't have to do much. You stand by a booth (that I'll make) and answer questions. I don't know anyone else whose dad is a tree doctor, so I'm sure you'll be a hit! You could bring pictures, maybe tools, too. And you could say how you got interested in it, and what the fun parts are.

　　Let's talk about it more later, okay? See you tonight!

Love,
Devon

1. Who wrote the note?
   - ○ A. Dad
   - ○ B. Devon
   - ○ C. the teacher

2. What is Dad's job?
   - ○ A. tollbooth worker
   - ○ B. eye doctor
   - ○ C. tree doctor

Sentence Mender

Rewrite the sentence to make it correct.

Can you reached up to the hiest shelf

☽ BrainTeaser ☾

The word bank lists words about community. Find and circle each word in the grid.

Word Bank

CITIZEN	CITY
VILLAGE	STREET
TOWN	URBAN
RURAL	NEIGHBOR

```
Q U V U U H P O C Z N
R R B T O O K A Q R E
U B W C I T E C S U I
R A E B U A M T D N G
A N S T R E E T S N H
L V I L L A G E K E B
Q Q C L F H M S A R O
R R I T L K Q T T T R
C I T I Z E N A E O M
D Y Y T O W N T T R A
```

Morning Jumpstarts: Reading, Grade 2 © 2013 Scholastic Teaching Resources

Name _____   Date _____

Morning Jumpstarts: Reading, Grade 2 © 2013 Scholastic Teaching Resources

WORD of the Day

calf: a young cow, seal, elephant, or whale

Use the word **calf** to tell which of those young animals you would most like to see.

_____

_____

FUN Phonics

Read each word pair. Circle pairs that rhyme.

1. fix box	2. jeep deep	3. Fred bread
4. grab glad	5. pink prince	6. arch birch
7. bench French	8. swift lift	9. champ chomp

Handwriting Helper

Read the *place* words. Trace each word. Then write it two times.

over

above

below

under

Ready, Set, READ!

Read. Then answer the questions.

The Dog *by Ogden Nash*
The truth I do not stretch or shove
When I state the dog is full of love.
I've also proved, by actual test,
A wet dog is the lovingest.

Rain *by Spike Milligan*
There are holes in the sky
Where the rain gets in,
But they're ever so small—
That's why rain is thin.

1. Which poet wrote about an animal? _____

2. How are the poems alike? _____

_____

3. *Lovingest* is not a real word. How do you know what it means?

_____

_____

Sentence Mender

Rewrite the sentence to make it correct.

Let's meat after school to trad baseball card

_____

❂ BrainTeaser ❂

The word bank lists words about rocks and minerals. Find and circle each word in the grid.

Word Bank

MINERAL	SAND
STONE	ROCK
GRAVEL	PEBBLE
COAL	GEM

```
G E M P E A C G O I
P R J E A H A S L G
T O Y B C C O A L R
C C P B S B D N L A
V K Z L J W F D V V
U P Y E P S T O N E
M I N E R A L S R L
G Y M R A C K H O O
Q J B S H O N E C G
```

34

Name _____ Date _____

WORD of the Day

plenty: all you need; more than enough

Use the word **plenty** to describe somewhere that has more than enough space.

_____

_____

FUN Phonics

Cross out the word that does *not* have a long-*a* phonogram. Then write a new word that uses the same phonogram.

1.   bake   lake   can   _____

2.   pan   mail   nail   _____

3.   clay   tray   had   _____

4.   gal   grate   chap   _____

Handwriting Helper

Read the *map* words. Trace each word. Then write it two times.

north _____ _____

south _____ _____

east _____ _____

west _____ _____

Ready, Set, READ!

Read. Then answer the questions.

"No dessert until you clean up your room!" said Dinah's dad.

Dinah got the message loud and clear. Yes, she wanted dessert and yes, her room was a mess. No more time for drawing cartoons. It was time to unclutter, or else.

Cleaning was not Dinah's best skill. Drawing was. She always kept her drawing table neat. She saved her best drawings in folders and in notebooks. It was everything else that she let pile up. She sat on a mountain of dirty clothes, toys, and old comics, wondering what to do.

Then she saw an empty laundry basket outside her room. *That's it!* she thought. *I'll throw all my junk into that basket and pile my dirty clothes on top. Then I'll carry the whole mess to the washing machine. Problem solved!*

1. What does *unclutter* mean?
   - ○ A. do laundry
   - ○ B. clean up
   - ○ C. climb a mountain

2. How did Dinah plan to clean up her room?

   _____

   _____

   _____

   _____

   _____

Sentence Mender

Rewrite the sentence to make it correct.

Our knew cows and horses eats fresh hey

_____

⦿ BrainTeaser ⦿

How many words can you list that rhyme with trash?

- 1–3 words = Good
- 4–6 words = Great
- 7–9 words = Super
- Over 10 words = You ROCK!

_____

_____

_____

Morning Jumpstarts: Reading, Grade 2 © 2013 Scholastic Teaching Resources

Name _____ Date _____

Morning Jumpstarts: Reading, Grade 2 © 2013 Scholastic Teaching Resources

WORD of the Day

arrive: to get to a place; to come

Use the word **arrive** to describe how you feel when you get to a favorite place.

_____

_____

FUN Phonics

Cross out the word that does *not* have a long-*e* phonogram. Then write a new word that uses the same phonogram.

1.  sell   deal   steal   _____

2.   bend   free   three   _____

3.   bleed   feed   set   _____

4.   tent   feel   heel   _____

Handwriting Helper

Read the *job* words. Trace each word. Then write it two times.

nurse _____

doctor _____

driver _____

pilot _____

📖 Ready, Set, READ!

Read. Then answer the questions.

Ouch! Don't squeeze so hard! That hurts! The angry pencil wiggled out of Jada's hand and fell to the floor. It bounced on its eraser, and then rolled under a bookcase. It stopped rolling when it bumped into a paper clip. "Why are you here?" asked the pencil. "Did that girl try to hurt you, too?"

"Oh, not at all," answered the paper clip. "But I hate getting bent and unbent, so I snuck away. I slid off a desk onto the floor and nobody came after me. Do you think there's any way we can get out of this place?"

The pencil peeked out. "I don't think so," it said. "Look at all those kids. Even if I got a big bounce from my eraser, one of them would most likely grab me."

1. What do you think Jada tried to do to the pencil?

_____

_____

_____

_____

_____

2. Where do you think the story takes place?
   ○ A. in jail
   ○ B. outside
   ○ C. in a classroom

Sentence Mender

Rewrite the sentence to make it correct.

mr gold drive A school bus

_____

⚙ BrainTeaser ⚙

How many words can you list that rhyme with **quill**?

- 1–3 words = Good
- 4–6 words = Great
- 7–9 words = Super
- Over 10 words = You ROCK!

_____

_____

Morning Jumpstarts: Reading, Grade 2 © 2013 Scholastic Teaching Resources

Name _____ Date _____

WORD of the Day

desert: dry area with few plants and little rain

Use the word **desert** to name a plant or animal that lives in such a place.

_____

_____

FUN Phonics

Cross out the word that does *not* have a long-*i* phonogram.
Then write a new word that uses the same phonogram.

1. lick   nice   slice   _____

2. hide   bread   wide   _____

3. light   fright   kit   _____

4. fly   tray   sky   _____

Handwriting Helper

Read the *family* words. Trace each word. Then write it two times.

father _____

mother _____

sister _____

brother _____

📖 Ready, Set, READ!

Read. Then answer the questions.

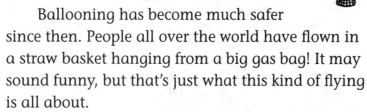

Hot-air balloons first carried people through the air over two centuries ago. Those early flights were short and risky. But people have always longed to fly, no matter how unsafe the idea seemed.

Ballooning has become much safer since then. People all over the world have flown in a straw basket hanging from a big gas bag! It may sound funny, but that's just what this kind of flying is all about.

Balloons come in many shapes and colors. You can see many kinds at balloon festivals. These outdoor events bring lots of hot-air balloon lovers to one place. They set up in an open field. They take off at about the same time. The sky fills with splashes of bright color. It's an amazing sight to see.

1. What is another name for the part of the balloon that holds air?
   - ○ A. basket
   - ○ B. gas bag
   - ○ C. straw

2. Why would people long ago risk flying in a balloon?

_____

_____

_____

_____

Sentence Mender

Rewrite the sentence to make it correct.

they went to the san diego zoo

_____

⑨ BrainTeaser ⑥

A picture pair can make you think of a *compound word*, like this:

Write the word the pictures make you think of.

= wheelchair

1.  + _____

2. + _____

3. + _____

40

Morning Jumpstarts: Reading, Grade 2 © 2013 Scholastic Teaching Resources

Name _____ Date _____

Morning Jumpstarts: Reading, Grade 2 © 2013 Scholastic Teaching Resources

WORD of the Day

honest: truthful; never lying or cheating

Use the word **honest** to tell why it's hard never to lie.

_____

_____

FUN Phonics

Cross out the word that does *not* have a long-*o* phonogram. Then write a new word that uses the same phonogram.

1. 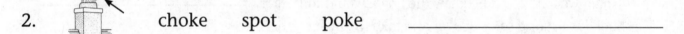 coat   float   box   _____

2. choke   spot   poke   _____

3. grow   cow   show   _____

4. phone   stone   bun   _____

Handwriting Helper

Read the *family* words. Trace each word. Then write it.

aunt

uncle

cousin

grandparent

Ready, Set, READ!

Read. Then answer the questions.

Hodja (HAWD-ja) and the Hawk　*A Turkish Folktale*

Liver was one of Hodja's favorite foods. He was happy when a friend sent him a recipe for a new liver dish. Hodja rode his donkey to the market to buy everything for the recipe. Last of all, he got the finest liver the butcher had to sell. He put the liver into his bag with the other things. Then he turned to ride home.

All Hodja could think about as he rode was the tasty liver dish. His mouth watered and his stomach was ready. Then in a flash, a hawk swooped down from the sky. The hawk stole the liver from Hodja's bag and flew off. Hodja tried to chase the bird, but of course it was no use.

Hodja was mad, but he knew the hawk would fail. He shook his fist and said, "Go on and take the liver. But you didn't get the recipe!"

1. Which is the job of a butcher?
   ○ A. to test recipes
   ○ B. to train birds
   ○ C. to sell meat

2. What tells you that Hodja is a funny character?

   _____

   _____

   _____

   _____

Sentence Mender

Rewrite the sentence to make it correct.

We will land in one our in portland, maine.

_____

◉ BrainTeaser ◉

Write the words from the word bank in ABC order in the rows of the grid. Then read down the column on the far right. Read the word that means *not on time*.

RIVER
CHART
WINDY
PASTA
THIRD

The word is _____.

42

Name _____ Date _____

WORD of the Day

suppose: to believe, expect, or imagine

Use the word **suppose** to describe what might happen at a birthday party.

_____

_____

FUN Phonics

Circle the word that has a long-*u* phonogram.
Then write a new word that uses the same phonogram.

1. hub   tube   cub   _____

2. round   took   blue   _____

3. mute   blood   cut   _____

4. fun   chew   cloud   _____

Handwriting Helper

Read the *art* words. Trace each word. Then write it two times.

draw

paint

sketch

picture

📖 Ready, Set, READ!

Read. Then answer the questions.

Tom got a new clock for his room. It looked like a spaceship. The clock had big red numbers on it.

Mom set the alarm for him. "Tom, your clock will get you up for school. I set it to ring at seven," she said. "Press on the tip of the spaceship to make the ringer stop." Tom touched the tip. "Yes, that's the spot. Now good night, son." Mom kissed Tom and turned out his light.

Tom liked seeing the numbers in the dark. Tom watched them change as his tired eyes closed. He dreamed about riding in a red spaceship.

Tom woke up by himself before seven. He waited for the clock to ring. He watched the numbers change. 6:58, 6:59, 7:00!

The ringer rang out. Tom loved its loud clang. But Tom did not press on the tip. He wanted to hear how long the ringing would last.

1. What does Tom's new clock look like?
   - ○ A. a watch
   - ○ B. a bell
   - ○ C. a spaceship

2. What time did Mom set the alarm to ring?

_____

Sentence Mender

Rewrite the sentence to make it correct.

I was born on monday, june 9, write?

_____

🌀 BrainTeaser 🌀

Write the words from the word bank in ABC order in the rows of the grid. Then read down the middle column. Read the word that names a color.

| TOWER |
| PHOTO |
| ELBOW |
| VENUS |
| HORNS |

The color is _____.

Morning Jumpstarts: Reading, Grade 2 © 2013 Scholastic Teaching Resources

Name _____ Date _____

Morning Jumpstarts: Reading, Grade 2 © 2013 Scholastic Teaching Resources

---

WORD of the Day

blizzard: a heavy snowstorm with strong winds

Use the word **blizzard** to write why traveling is hard in that kind of storm.

_____

_____

FUN Phonics

Circle the correct spelling of the word for each picture. Then copy it.

1.   soot   sut   suit   _____

2.   to   two   too   _____

3.   roof   rough   rewf   _____

4.   sup   soup   soop   _____

Handwriting Helper

Read the *contrast* words. Trace each word. Then write it.

different _____

opposite _____

instead _____

unlike

📖 Ready, Set, READ!

Read. Then answer the questions.

My dad taught me to make my favorite breakfast. He called it a Texas egg. But my dad never went to Texas, and he couldn't cook any other dish.

What is a Texas egg? You might know it as toad in the hole or egg in a basket. It's easy to cook. Dad helped me make my first one when I was eight years old. First you tear a hole in the middle of a slice of bread. Then you melt some butter in a frying pan and put the bread  in for a bit. Next you crack an egg into the hole. When the egg begins to get hard, you flip the whole thing over. That way, both sides can cook.

So a Texas egg is a fried egg and toast rolled into one! But how did it get that name? My dad always said it looked like a Texas flag.

1. How did the writer learn to make a Texas egg?

_____

_____

_____

2. In what way is the Texas flag like this breakfast dish?

_____

_____

_____

_____

_____

Sentence Mender

Rewrite the sentence to make it correct.

we marches in a parade on new year's day

_____

🌀 BrainTeaser 🌀

Each piece of clothing below is missing its vowels. Write *a*, *e*, *i*, *o*, or *u* to finish spelling each one.

1. d r _____ s s

2. s _____ c k s

3. s c _____ r f

4. s h _____ r t

5. j _____ c k _____ t

6. j _____ _____ n s

46

Morning Jumpstarts: Reading, Grade 2 © 2013 Scholastic Teaching Resources

Name _____ Date _____

WORD of the Day

sparkle: twinkle; shine brightly; be lively

Use the word **sparkle** to describe something in nature.

_____

_____

FUN Phonics

Read each word in the word bank.
Write it where it goes in the vowel chart.

Word Bank

foam	fruit	tray	child
sigh	both	pie	heat
flake	tune	free	cute

Long *a*	Long *e*	Long *i*	Long *o*	Long *u*

Handwriting Helper

Read the *money* words. Trace each word. Then write it two times.

coin

cent

penny

nickel

Ready, Set, READ!

Read. Then answer the questions.

The Zapotec [zah-puh-TEK] people lived in Mexico long before Columbus got to the "New World." The Zapotec were famous weavers. They made wool rugs by hand. Each rug took skill and many months of work.

Weavers first gathered wool from sheep. They cleaned the wool and spun it into yarn. Then they dyed the yarn many colors.

The dyes once came from materials found in the area. Red came from crushed insects found on cactus plants. Brown and tan came from roots, bark, and nuts. Plants and flowers were used to make blue, green, and yellow.

Most Zapotec rugs had patterns with pictures. These pictures stood for things such as wind, rain, snails, candles, and teeth.

1. What was the main material used to make Zapotec rugs?
   - ○ A. cotton
   - ○ B. flowers
   - ○ C. wool

2. Why did it take so long to weave a rug?

   _____

   _____

   _____

   _____

   _____

   _____

Sentence Mender

Rewrite the sentence to make it correct.

Cannt you sea the kitten on the roof

_____

☺ BrainTeaser ☺

Each animal below is missing its vowels.
Write *a*, *e*, *i*, *o*, or *u* to finish spelling each one.

1. w h ____ l ____

2. l ____ ____ n

3. t ____ g ____ r

4. p ____ n d ____

5. r ____ b b ____ t

6. m ____ n k ____ y

Morning Jumpstarts: Reading, Grade 2 © 2013 Scholastic Teaching Resources

Name _____ Date _____

WORD of the Day

predict: to tell what may happen; forecast

Use the word **predict** to write what you might do when you grow up.

_____

_____

FUN Phonics

The letters **oo** can have two different sounds.
$\overline{oo}$ stands for long *oo*, as in **m<u>oo</u>n**.
$\breve{oo}$ stands for short *oo*, as in **b<u>oo</u>k**.
Say each word in the word bank.
Write it in the chart where it belongs.

Word Bank

cook	spoon
fool	foot
hood	room

$\overline{oo}$ as in *moon* 🌙	$\breve{oo}$ as in *book* 📖

Handwriting Helper

Read the *money* words. Trace each word. Then write it two times.

dime

quarter

dollar

bank

Ready, Set, READ!

Read. Then answer the questions.

It was a clear night. Nick carried his telescope (TELL-uh-skope) out to the backyard. As he set it up, he gazed into the sky. He looked for the brightest star he could see with his own eyes. Once he picked one, he aimed his telescope at it.

Nick looked at the star he picked. He couldn't believe his eyes. The bright star looked light rusty red. But it was no star, it was the planet Mars. How did Nick know? How could he *not* know! He was reading a bright sign on it that said, "Hello from Mars!"

Nick rubbed his eyes. Then he looked again at Mars. This time the sign said, "Mars to Nick. We need you here. Expect a spaceship to pick you up at midnight tomorrow. Pack Earth food and pajamas."

1. Which would make the best title for this story?
   O A. Nick Gets a Telescope
   O B. Next Stop, Mars!
   O C. Packing for a Trip

2. What do you think Nick will do?

   _____

   _____

   _____

   _____

   _____

   _____

Sentence Mender

Rewrite the sentence to make it correct.

I didint see the dogs tale under my chair.

_____

☺ BrainTeaser ☺

Put each group of words in order to make a sentence.
Start each sentence with a capital letter. Use an end mark.

1. eyes your open　　_____

2. wash must up she　　_____

3. cat like you my do　　_____

Morning Jumpstarts: Reading, Grade 2 © 2013 Scholastic Teaching Resources

Name _____ Date _____

Morning Jumpstarts: Reading, Grade 2 © 2013 Scholastic Teaching Resources

WORD of the Day

danger: something that harms or hurts; risk

Use the word **danger** to write about something that can harm or hurt small children.

_____

_____

FUN Phonics

Each sentence below needs an **ar** word and an **or** word.
Read the words that start each row.
Write them in the blanks so each sentence makes sense.

1. car shore   Al drove the _____ to the sea _____.

2. sharp thorns   The _____ on a rose are very _____.

3. farm corn   We pick _____ at a local _____.

4. hard sport   Is the _____ of golf _____ for kids?

5. smart horse   How do I know if a _____ is _____?

Handwriting Helper

Read the *order* words. Trace each word. Then write it two times.

first

second

third

fourth

Ready, Set, READ!

Read. Then answer the questions.

Why Sun and Moon Live in the Sky   *A Myth From Nigeria*

Sun married Moon and they built a house together. Sun said goodbye to Water. "Dear friend, please visit us soon."

"Thank you, Sun! But I would need to bring all my people with me. Is your house big enough?" asked Water.

Sun said, "Ah! We will build a bigger house." So Sun and Moon built a very large house, the biggest in the world.

Sun and Moon were eager for Water's visit. They could hear Water gurgling and sloshing before they saw him.

Water began to flow in to Sun and Moon's house with all his people. As they filled the house halfway, Water asked if the house was safe. Moon said, "Keep coming!"

When Water reached the roof, he asked, "May we still keep coming?"

"Of course!" said Sun and Moon, who moved onto the roof. As more of Water's people came, Sun and Moon moved into the sky—where they are today.

1. Why was Water unsure about visiting Sun and Moon at first?
   - ○ A. Water missed them.
   - ○ B. Water didn't like their house.
   - ○ C. Their house might not be big enough.

2. Which word best describes Sun and Moon?
   - ○ A. nervous
   - ○ B. welcoming
   - ○ C. worried

Sentence Mender

Rewrite the sentence to make it correct.

Her will come stay with us for two weaks.

๑ BrainTeaser ๑

Fill in the chart to make each word plural. Use *–s* or *–es*.
Two are done for you.

One	More Than One	One	More Than One
1. cow	cows	4. beach	beaches
2. wish		5. spoon	
3. mess		6. shape	

Morning Jumpstarts: Reading, Grade 2 © 2013 Scholastic Teaching Resources

Name _____ Date _____

WORD of the Day

sturdy: strong, hardy; solidly made; built to last

Use the word **sturdy** to write why a builder needs a strong and solid ladder.

_____

_____

FUN Phonics

Each word in the word bank has an **ur** sound spelled with **er**, **ir**, or **ur**. Write each word in the chart where it belongs.

Word Bank

girl	fern	burn
germ	fur	first
stir	hurt	serve

h**er**d	b**ir**d	n**ur**se

Handwriting Helper

Read the *order* words. Trace each word. Then write it two times.

fifth _____

sixth _____

seventh _____

eighth _____

Morning Jumpstarts: Reading, Grade 2 © 2013 Scholastic Teaching Resources

Ready, Set, READ!

Read. Then answer the questions.

"A statue to a dog?" asked Dad.

Kurt begged to go to Central Park in New York City for the big event. "Not just any dog! Balto was a hero. And New York is the first city to honor a dog!"

Kurt read everything he could about Balto. A deadly disease hit a small Alaska town in January of 1925. The nearest medicine was hundreds of miles away.

Kurt went on. "Doctors sent medicine by dogsled. The dogs and mushers raced day and night. It took over five days, but they got there and saved lives. Let's go see this real-life hero."

Kurt changed his dad's mind. Dad closed his office on December 17, 1925. He and Kurt went to Central Park. They stood on a hill. From there they smiled down on the real Balto and on his new statue.

1. Who was Balto?
   - O A. a doctor
   - O B. a pilot
   - O C. a sled dog

2. What do you think *mushers* do?
   - O A. drive sled dogs
   - O B. make medicine
   - O C. build statues

Sentence Mender

Rewrite the sentence to make it correct.

Lets play checkers i will take red.

⊙ BrainTeaser ⊙

Fill in the chart to make each word singular.
The first one is done for you.

More Than One	One	More Than One	One
1. feet	foot	4. teeth	
2. men		5. children	
3. heroes		6. foxes	

Morning Jumpstarts: Reading, Grade 2 © 2013 Scholastic Teaching Resources

Name _____ Date _____

Morning Jumpstarts: Reading, Grade 2 © 2013 Scholastic Teaching Resources

WORD of the Day

flutter: to wave or flap quickly; to beat faster

Use the word **flutter** to describe something that makes your heart beat faster.

_____

_____

FUN Phonics

When **y** is a vowel, it can sound like **long e** or **long i**. Read each word. Write **e** or **i** to tell which sound of **y** you hear.

1. fly	2. fifty	3. jelly
long ____	long ____	long ____
4. cry	5. dry	6. strawberry
long ____	long ____	long ____

Handwriting Helper

Read the words for footwear. Trace each word. Then write it two times.

shoes

boots

sandals

sneakers

Ready, Set, READ!

Read. Then answer the questions.

Al's neighborhood didn't have many trees or green spaces. It did have an empty lot full of weeds. So one spring day, Al borrowed some tools and asked his friends to a garden party.

"A garden party!" said Tyesha. "Where?"

"In a garden we'll make ourselves!" said Al.

Saturday morning, a dozen people showed up at the weedy lot and got busy. They pulled out the weeds. They cleared out trash. The empty lot slowly became an open space. No garden yet, but it was a start.

Sunday, 14 people came. Ramon borrowed a hand tiller, a digging machine to churn up the soil. People took turns using it because it was hard work. In a few hours, the empty lot was different again. Still no garden, but Al would bring in fresh, rich soil on Monday.

1. How did Ramon use the tiller?
   - O A. to cut down weeds
   - O B. to dig up soil
   - O C. to haul away trash

2. Why did Al take on this project?

   _____

   _____

   _____

   _____

   _____

   _____

Sentence Mender

Rewrite the sentence to make it correct.

hes mom leaves for work at six oclock in the morning.

_____

⊚ BrainTeaser ⊚

A *synonym* is a word that means the same or almost the same as another word.

Write a synonym from the word bank for each bolded word.

1. **throw** the ball   _____

2. **complete** the book   _____

3. **noisy** horn   _____

| loud |
| toss |
| finish |

56

Morning Jumpstarts: Reading, Grade 2 © 2013 Scholastic Teaching Resources

Name _____ Date _____

<table>
<tr><td>**WORD of the Day**</td><td>**meadow**: a grassy field where animals eat

Use the word **meadow** to describe some sights and sounds in one.</td></tr>
</table>

_____

_____

FUN Phonics

The *schwa* /ə/ is a quick sound with no accent.
Schwa has the **uh** sound as in **alone**. Circle the word
in each pair that begins with the schwa sound.

1. alarm acted	2. anger again	3. adding adult
4. agree ashes	5. asking awake	6. asleep army
7. aim ago	8. able about	9. apple apart

Handwriting Helper

Read the *how much* words. Trace each word. Then write it.

always

often

sometimes

never

Morning Jumpstarts: Reading, Grade 2 © 2013 Scholastic Teaching Resources

Ready, Set, READ!

Read. Then answer the questions.

Rita woke up with a start. Her little clock said 1:30. It was the middle of the night. Rita was usually a sound sleeper. So why was she wide awake at this hour?

She rubbed her eyes and sat up. She didn't hear anything but her dad snoring. Just then, Rita noticed a funny smell. What was it? It tickled her nose and made the back of her throat feel a little scratchy. Rita leaped out of bed just as the smoke alarm went off. Its loud sound hurt her ears—but for a good reason.

Rita raced to wake her parents. "Get up! I think there's a fire in our house!" she yelled. Mom grabbed her phone and dialed 911 for help. Dad wrapped Rita in a blanket and hurried out the back door with her. Mom swooped up the cat in a tote bag. They all stood in the yard, looking at the smoke coming from the attic window . . .

1. What does it mean to be a *sound sleeper?*

   _____

   _____

   _____

   _____

2. Why did Dad wrap Rita in a blanket?
   - A. to save the blanket
   - B. to let her sleep
   - C. to protect her from smoke

Sentence Mender

Rewrite the sentence to make it correct.

Randys new house have too floors.

_____

☺ BrainTeaser ☺

A *synonym* is a word that means the same or almost the same as another word.

Write a synonym for each word.

1. hurry = _____   3. timid = _____

2. mend = _____   4. sleepy = _____

58

Morning Jumpstarts: Reading, Grade 2 © 2013 Scholastic Teaching Resources

Name _____ Date _____

WORD of the Day

eager: wanting to; very interested in; ready

Use the word **eager** to write about something new you hope to try.

_____

_____

FUN Phonics

C can have two different sounds.

Soft *c* sounds like /s/, as in <u>c</u>ity. Hard *c* sounds like /k/, as in <u>c</u>amp.

Read each word. Write **S** or **H** to show whether you hear a **Hard** *c* or **Soft** *c*.

1. cup _____	2. center _____	3. uncle _____
4. place _____	5. camel _____	6. fence _____
7. claw _____	8. magic _____	9. celery _____

Handwriting Helper

Read the words about writing. Trace each word. Then write it.

story

poem

fiction

nonfiction

JUMPSTART 26

📖 Ready, Set, READ!

Read. Then answer the questions.

The winters are cold and snowy where Tina lives. Ice hockey is a big sport there. Many kids learn to skate as soon as they can balance, as soon as they aren't afraid to fall. Which they will!

Tina first asked for ice skates when she was four. Her older brother was already skating, and she didn't want to be left out. Her parents were glad to grant her wish. They got her pink skates. She got purple pads for her knees and elbows. She got a pink safety helmet. Her first skate would be at the town ice rink. Her brother would hold her hand.

Tina grinned as she took her first wobbly steps on the ice. Her dad offered to borrow an ice walker. It's a light frame that slides. "No thanks," said Tina. "I've got my brother." After five minutes, Tina let go of Gary's hand. She wanted to skate by herself.

1. Who is Gary?
   - ○ A. Tina's dad
   - ○ B. Tina's coach
   - ○ C. Tina's brother

2. Why did Tina want to skate at such a young age?
   - ○ A. She wanted to be like her brother.
   - ○ B. It was too cold to do anything else.
   - ○ C. Tina liked all kinds of sports.

Sentence Mender

Rewrite the sentence to make it correct.

Maria askd if she could use dads tool kit

_____

🌀 BrainTeaser 🌀

A *synonym* is a word that means the same or almost the same as another word.

Write a synonym for each word.

1. friend = _____

2. cure = _____

3. choose = _____

4. simple = _____

Morning Jumpstarts: Reading, Grade 2 © 2013 Scholastic Teaching Resources

Name _____ Date _____

ΔΦΔΦΔΦΔΦΔΦΔΦΔΦΔΦΔΦ

WORD of the Day

explain: to give a reason for something

Use the word **explain** to write a question you could ask.

_____

_____

FUN Phonics

G can have two different sounds.

Soft *g* sounds like /j/, as in **gem**. Hard *g* sounds like /g/, as in **game**.

Read each word. Write **S** or **H** to show whether you hear a **Soft** *g* or **Hard** *g*.

1. gown _____	2. gym _____	3. giant _____
4. goose _____	5. huge _____	6. ginger _____
7. gentle _____	8. guess _____	9. orange _____

Handwriting Helper

Read the *job* words. Trace each word. Then write it two times.

actor

dancer

clerk

cashier

Ready, Set, READ!

Read. Then answer the questions.

The Fairy Tulips   *An English Fairy Tale*

A kind old woman spent most of her time in her garden. She loved all living things. Most of all, she loved her pink tulips.

She woke up one night at midnight. She heard soft singing and babies cooing. She looked out her window. The sounds seemed to come from the tulips. But she could not see anyone, so she went back to sleep.

The next day the old woman walked through her pink tulips. She saw nothing special. But that night she again woke up at midnight. Again she heard soft singing and babies cooing.

She got up and tiptoed outside. Her tulips were swaying gently. But there was no wind! Then her eyes opened wide. A small fairy mother stood in the tulips, singing. She rocked the tulips like tiny cradles. And inside each tulip lay a cooing fairy baby.

The woman tiptoed home. From then on, she never picked another tulip.

1. What is another word for *swaying*?
   - O A. singing
   - O B. rocking
   - O C. cooing

2. Why did the old woman stop picking her tulips?

   _____

   _____

   _____

   _____

   _____

   _____

Sentence Mender

Rewrite the sentence to make it correct.

Jack end Jill carrys a pail of water.

_____

☉ BrainTeaser ☉

Write the *opposite* of each **bolded** word below. Use the word bank.

1. **awake** by eight   _____

2. will never **sink**   _____

3. **frown** at us   _____

4. **winter** clothes   _____

Word Bank
float
smile
asleep
summer

62

Name _____ Date _____

WORD of the Day

dwelling: a place to live; home; shelter

Use the word **dwelling** to describe a place where you would like to live.

_____

_____

FUN Phonics

Write an exact rhyme for each word below.
Start with an *r* blend from the box.
Use each blend at least once.

> **r Blends**
>
> br   cr   dr   fr
> gr   pr   tr

1. doom _____	2. mesh _____	3. wisp _____
4. book _____	5. lift _____	6. tapes _____
7. must _____	8. thank _____	9. stump _____

Handwriting Helper

Read the words that tell where. Trace each word. Then write it two times.

behind _____

beside _____

between _____

through _____

📖 Ready, Set, READ!

Read. Then answer the questions.

You have blood that moves around inside your body. If you get a cut, some blood can spill out. Earth, too, has liquids that move around deep inside. From time to time, the Earth's liquid can spill out. No bandage can stop it!

Magma (MAHG-ma) is thick, hot, liquid rock. It is found inside Earth, miles below layers of rock. We can't feel it on land, but the layers can move and slide. Cracks open up. The moving rocks can squeeze the magma up through those cracks. What happens when that hot magma bursts out? That is an erupting volcano!

A volcano is any mountain that lets magma get out. When magma gets to the surface, scientists call it lava. Lava is so hot, it can burn up everything it touches. It can move quickly or slowly. When it finally cools off, it becomes new rock.

1. In what way is magma like blood?
   - ○ A. It comes out of a volcano.
   - ○ B. It is liquid and can spill out.
   - ○ C. A bandage can stop it.

2. When magma gets to the surface, scientists call it
   - ○ A. a volcano
   - ○ B. layers
   - ○ C. lava

Sentence Mender

Rewrite the sentence to make it correct.

My favorite numbers are for, seven eleven and sixtine

_____

๑ BrainTeaser ๑

Write another word to finish each side of the opposites box.
Examples are done for you.

loud	quiet		smooth	rough
noisy				bumpy

Morning Jumpstarts: Reading, Grade 2 © 2013 Scholastic Teaching Resources

Name _____ Date _____

Morning Jumpstarts: Reading, Grade 2 © 2013 Scholastic Teaching Resources

WORD of the Day

mammoth: very big; huge; gigantic

Use the word **mammoth** to write about a huge animal.

_____

_____

FUN Phonics

Write an *l* blend from the box in front of each phonogram to make a word.

l Blends

bl cl fl
gl pl sl

1. _____ ace	2. _____ ea	3. _____ ove
4. _____ ade	5. _____ eep	6. _____ ick
7. _____ oom	8. _____ ue	9. _____ ush

Handwriting Helper

Read the *school* words. Trace each word. Then write it.

pupil

student

teacher

classroom

Ready, Set, READ!

Read. Then answer the questions.

"You're such a bookworm!" teased Jed. "Use the computer with me."

"No thanks," said Traci. "I'd rather pick a biography. I love reading about the lives of real people." Traci sat on a pillow in the biography section. She wondered who to read about. She spread nine books out the floor near her, all from the *H* shelf.

Suddenly, the library went dark. "Turn the lights back on, please!" Traci called out, but no lights went on. She came out of her corner into the dark library. The teachers and kids were gone. The lights were off. Worst of all, the door was locked.

Traci banged on the door, but no one came. She tried to use the intercom on the wall, but it didn't work. Now what? she thought. So she went back to her corner to look at those biographies on the floor. She picked *Mr. Houdini, Escape Artist*.

1. A *bookworm* is somebody who
   - ○ A. reads a lot.
   - ○ B. likes science.
   - ○ C. eats the pages of books.

2. How do you know that Houdini was a real person?

   _____

   _____

   _____

   _____

   _____

   _____

Sentence Mender

Rewrite the sentence to make it correct.

The winners where tom billy jake lynda.

_____

๑ BrainTeaser ๏

Write another word to finish each side of the opposites box.
Examples are done for you.

break	repair		fast	slow
	mend			quick

Morning Jumpstarts: Reading, Grade 2 © 2013 Scholastic Teaching Resources

Name _____ Date _____

WORD of the Day

relax: to loosen up; rest; make less tense

Use the word **relax** to write about one way you like to unwind after school.

_____

_____

FUN Phonics

Solve each riddle by writing a word that starts with an *s* blend from the box.

s Blends
sc sl sm
sp st sw

1. Not large? _____	2. Move in water? _____
3. Part of a shirt? _____	4. Sky twinkler? _____
5. Say *BOO!* _____	6. Go bad? _____

Handwriting Helper

Read the *room* words. Trace each word. Then write it two times.

gym

kitchen

library

bedroom

📖 Ready, Set, READ!

Read. Then answer the questions.

Mrs. Ives stood in front of the class. "Today is writing day, boys and girls. I'd like you to write about something that really happened to you. The story can be on any subject, as long as it's true and you are in it. Please check that your story has a beginning, middle, and end."

Hal raised his hand. "Can we write about sports?"

"If you have a true story about sports, that's fine," said Mrs. Ives. "You know, class, I'm a big sports fan. I'll enjoy any sports stories you have to write."

The class got busy writing. Most did choose to write sports stories. Seda wrote about a soccer game she won. Vera described learning to swim. Ed's story was about his best bowling game.

When it was time to read the stories aloud, Hal asked to go first. He stood up and read, "Rain. No Game. The End."

1. How did Hal's question help the class?

_____

_____

_____

_____

2. What do you think of Hal's story?

_____

_____

_____

_____

Sentence Mender

Rewrite the sentence to make it correct.

Are teacher is reading *Mr. Peabodys Apples* to us.

_____

⟲ BrainTeaser ⟳

Fill in the chart with kinds of **toys**, **foods**, and **animals**. The letters above each column tell the first letter for each word in it. Two words are done for you.

	B	L	S	T
Toys			scooter	
Foods		lettuce		
Animals				

Morning Jumpstarts: Reading, Grade 2 © 2013 Scholastic Teaching Resources

Name _____ Date _____

╔═══════════════════════╗
WORD of the Day
╚═══════════════════════╝

distance: how far it is between two things; a place far away

Use the word **distance** to write about something you can see from far away.

_____

_____

FUN Phonics

Copy the word for each picture. Underline its final blend.

1.	dusk desk disk	2.	gust grant gift	3.	stamp stump scalp
_____		_____		_____	
4.	cold cord colt	5.	quiet quart quilt	6.	held hump hand
_____		_____		_____	

Handwriting Helper

Read the *sense* words. Trace each word. Then write it two times.

smell _____

touch _____

taste _____

sight _____

Ready, Set, READ!

Read. Then answer the questions.

How Bluebirds Got to Be Blue   *A Pima Indian Tale*

Long ago, bluebirds had dull feathers without color. They were not the bright blue like they are now. This is how they got to be blue.

One day, two dull bluebirds were flying around chasing each other. They flew far from their home. From high in the sky, they saw a lake they had never seen before. It was a sparkling, shining blue. The birds so loved the color they decided to dive into it. They swam and splashed and sang out their wish.

Blue lake water is so blue
Let's stay in 'til we're blue, too!

The two birds returned to the lake each morning for three days to swim and splash and sing. On the fourth day, they flapped their wings and their dull feathers shook loose and sank. New sleek blue feathers grew in their place. "We have freshened our feathers!" they chirped with joy. And bluebirds have been blue ever since.

1. What is the main idea of this tale?

_____

_____

_____

_____

_____

2. Which word is the opposite of *dull*?
   O A. blue
   O B. bright
   O C. loose

Sentence Mender

Rewrite the sentence to make it correct.

We don't got no shoo polish.

_____

⑨ BrainTeaser ⑥

The sentence in the box has only four words. But every word starts with the *same* letter. Write a sentence in which every word starts with **s**. Make it as long as you can.

| **B**en **b**ites **b**ig **b**erries. |

_____

Morning Jumpstarts: Reading, Grade 2 © 2013 Scholastic Teaching Resources

Name _____ Date _____

WORD of the Day

homesick: feeling sad to be far from home

What do you get **homesick** for when you are away? Use the word to write about it.

_____

_____

FUN Phonics

Copy the word for each picture. Underline its final blend.

1. drink drift dump _____	2. test tent tend _____	3. bird boast board _____
4. stark short shark _____	5. chunk chest champ _____	6. wart wasp wind _____

Handwriting Helper

Read the *v* words. Trace each word. Then write it two times.

vanilla

village

voice

voyage

 # Ready, Set, READ!

Read. Then answer the questions.

All living things need food to stay alive. Most plants get what they need from the sun, rain, and soil. But some plants must eat meat to stay alive. The Venus flytrap is this kind of plant.

Venus flytraps grow in wet, sunny spots. They live in North and South Carolina. The soil there is sandy, so they cannot get all they need. This is why they have a mouth and stomach all in one!

The Venus flytrap gets meat in a clever way. It gives off a sweet smell which invites a bug to drop by. But when the bug gets in the leaves, they close around it like a trap door.

The bug is trapped. It can't get out, and nothing else can get in. The leaves give off juices that melt the bug into food for the plant.

1. How is the Venus flytrap unlike most other plants?
   ○ A. It has no flowers.
   ○ B. It needs no water.
   ○ C. It eats meat.

2. Why would a bug ever come near a Venus flytrap?

   _____

   _____

   _____

   _____

   _____

Sentence Mender

Rewrite the sentence to make it correct.

Jack might tomorro be late?

_____

☺ BrainTeaser ☺

The sentence in the box has only five words. But every word starts with the *same* letter. Write a sentence in which every word starts with **t**. Make it as long as you can.

> **C**asey **c**alls **c**ousin **C**lara **C**ortez.

_____

_____

Morning Jumpstarts: Reading, Grade 2 © 2013 Scholastic Teaching Resources

Name _____ Date _____

WORD of the Day

cluster: to stand or grow near; gather in a group

Use the word **cluster** to tell why children might gather near a window.

_____

_____

FUN Phonics

Write the missing consonant digraph so that each phrase makes sense.

> **Consonant Digraphs**
>
> ch ph sh th wh

1. fried _____ icken	2. window _____ ade
3. dad's cell _____ one	4. ten, twenty, _____ irty
5. when and _____ ere	6. _____ ow and tell

Handwriting Helper

Read the *k* words. Trace each word. Then write it two times.

kayak

_____

kernel

_____

kneel

_____

knuckle

_____

Ready, Set, READ!

Read. Then answer the questions.

"I'm not making noise. I'm making music!" said Ivy. She sat at the piano with a music notebook by her side. She played different tunes on the keys. When she got the notes just right, she wrote them down in her book. It was slow work, but Ivy loved doing it.

Her brother Ron teased her. "Ivy," he said, "other people have already written all the music we will ever need!"

"That's not the point," answered Ivy. "I hear songs in my head that nobody else knows. They are new songs I make up. I'm a composer. Composers write music, but not because the world needs it. It's because the music is inside our heads and wants to get out!"

Ron rolled his eyes and left. Ivy kept working on her song. Then she set up her notebook on the piano rack. She played her new song from start to end. Then she began to think of words for her tune.

1. What is the work of a composer?
   - A. writing poems
   - B. painting pictures
   - C. making new music

2. What does Ron think about Ivy's work?

   _____

   _____

   _____

   _____

   _____

   _____

Sentence Mender

Rewrite the sentence to make it correct.

Dad mist the train by a hole hour!

_____

🌀 BrainTeaser 🌀

The sentence in the box has only five words. But the first letters in the words are in ABC order. Write your own sentence like that. Start the first word with **L**.

> **D**izzy **e**lephants **f**ind **g**reen **h**ippos.

_____

_____

Morning Jumpstarts: Reading, Grade 2 © 2013 Scholastic Teaching Resources

Name _____ Date _____

| WORD of the Day | **aircraft**: any machine that can fly

Use the word **aircraft** to write about one you'd like to fly in, and why. |

_____

_____

FUN Phonics

Write the ending consonant digraph so that each sentence makes sense.

> **Consonant Digraphs**
>
> ch gh ng ph sh th

1. My cold makes me cou_____.	2. A bar gra_____ shows data.
3. What a juicy pea_____!	4. Let's si_____ a lively tune.
5. Mario lost another too_____.	6. Please feed the goldfi_____.

Handwriting Helper

Read the words with *x*. Trace each one. Then write it two times.

x-ray

wax

fix

mailbox

Morning Jumpstarts: Reading, Grade 2 © 2013 Scholastic Teaching Resources

Ready, Set, READ!

Read. Then answer the questions.

Did you ever get a headache from eating cold things fast? You're not alone. This happens to many people. Here's what is going on.

A "brain freeze" happens when something very cold touches the roof of your mouth. Ice cream and other cold foods can cause this. So much cold at once shrinks your blood vessels. The brain gets surprised, blood flow slows down, and you may start to hurt.

The good news is that a brain freeze doesn't last long. The pain goes away by itself. Doctors say to press the tongue to the roof of the mouth. This warms up the area and things get back to normal.

The best way to avoid a brain freeze is to enjoy cold or icy things slowly. Take itty-bitty bites, little licks, and small sips. Then you will have all the fun of cooling off with none of the pain!

1. What causes a brain freeze?

_____

_____

_____

_____

_____

_____

2. Where is the *roof* of your mouth?
   ○ A. near the side
   ○ B. by the tongue
   ○ C. at the top

Sentence Mender

Rewrite the sentence to make it correct.

Mr. davis is The New Principal of my school.

_____

⑨ BrainTeaser ⑥

Each sentence below has one *extra* word. Find it and cross it out.

1. The street lamps come over on at night.

2. Who has with the last piece of the puzzle?

3. You can because use my ruler to measure your desk.

4. Waves water splash onto the rocky beach.

Morning Jumpstarts: Reading, Grade 2 © 2013 Scholastic Teaching Resources

Name _____ Date _____

WORD of the Day

shelter: a safe place that protects against bad weather or danger

Use the word to write why some cats or dogs live in an animal **shelter**.

_____

_____

FUN Phonics

The letters **ng** can be in the middle or at the end of a word.
Each picture stands for a word with **ng**. Write the word.

1. _____	2. _____	3. _____
4. _____	5. _____	6. _____

Handwriting Helper

Read the *j* words. Trace each one. Then write it two times.

jewel _____

judge _____

janitor _____

jockey _____

Ready, Set, READ!

Read. Then answer the questions.

Mama was making a big pancake. Her six children begged for tastes. "Not yet. We must wait for the pancake to flip itself," said Mama.

The pancake heard this and got scared. "Six little mouths will not eat me!" it said. The pancake jumped out of the pan and rolled out the door. The children yelled, "Stop!" But the pancake rolled fast and into the woods.

The pancake rolled past a fox. "Pancake, where are you going?" the fox asked. The pancake saw the sharp teeth the fox had. So it kept on rolling without saying a word. The pancake passed a rabbit, a deer, and an owl. But it never spoke and would not stop.

Soon the pancake got tired. It slowed down near a hut. "Oh, pancake!" said a cat. "You look thirsty. Come share my water." The pancake did feel hot and dry. So it rolled up to the cat. What will happen next?

1. What kind of story is this?
   ○ A. folktale
   ○ B. report
   ○ C. mystery

2. What do you think happens next?

   _____

   _____

   _____

   _____

   _____

Sentence Mender

Rewrite the sentence to make it correct.

She have a bad sore throat for to days.

_____

⑨ BrainTeaser ⑥

Think of two words for each word part in the chart.
Words can be any length.

Word part	Words
-ack	
-ame	
-ell	

Morning Jumpstarts: Reading, Grade 2 © 2013 Scholastic Teaching Resources

Name _____ Date _____

WORD of the Day

observe: to follow, watch, or notice; study

Use the word **observe** to write about something outside that catches your interest.

_____

_____

FUN Phonics

Circle all the words that have the *oy* sound.

1. boil	olive	enjoy	port	point
2. royal	coin	body	voice	small
3. Joyce	Troy	Leon	Leroy	Cody

Circle all the words that have the *ow* sound.

4. shout	coach	howl	cloud	grown
5. meow	crown	flute	pout	flower
6. allow	ouch	pillow	show	loud

Handwriting Helper
....

Read the *q* words. Trace each one. Then write it two times.

queen

_____

quiet

_____

question

_____

quickly

📖 Ready, Set, READ!

Read. Then answer the questions.

Our nation has three holidays for families. We have Mother's Day and Father's Day in the spring. We have Grandparents Day in the fall.

Every May 5 in Japan is another kind of family day. It is Children's Day. Japanese families honor their boys and girls on that day every year. They wish for them to be healthy and happy. They pray that they will grow up to be fine adults.

Children's Day in Japan has many customs. It always falls on the fifth day of the fifth month. A family flies a carp flag outside—one for each child. The carp is a fish that is strong in body and mind. Families set up dolls of great heroes inside.

The children play games, go to fairs, and take part in many other fun events. They get many gifts and treats. One of the best is a sticky rice cake filled with sweet paste.

1. When is Children's Day in Japan?
   - O A. March 5
   - O B. May 5
   - O C. May 15

2. Why is the carp a good sign for Children's Day?
   - O A. It is on a flag.
   - O B. The fish is tasty.
   - O C. The fish is strong in body and mind.

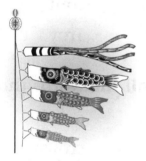

Sentence Mender

Rewrite the sentence to make it correct.

I finishd my lunch sew now ill play soccer.

_____

🌀 BrainTeaser 🌀

Each word below has two pairs of missing letters. Fill in the missing letter pairs. Use the letter bank. Each pair is used two times in the same word.

> **Letter Bank**
>
> ac   ar   nd
> oo   wn

1. b ____ ____ kp ____ ____ k

2. ha ____ ____ sta ____ ____

3. b ____ ____ ny ____ ____ d

4. do ____ ____ to ____ ____

Morning Jumpstarts: Reading, Grade 2 © 2013 Scholastic Teaching Resources

Name _____ Date _____

WORD of the Day

gritty: brave; able to keep going

Use the word **gritty** to describe a character from a book or movie.

_____

_____

FUN Phonics

Draw lines to match the *contraction* with two words that mean the same. The first one is done for you.

won't •	• cannot
can't •	• is not
didn't •	• does not
isn't •	• did not
doesn't •	• are not
haven't •	• will not
wouldn't •	• would not
aren't •	• have not

Contract means *to get smaller.*

Handwriting Helper

Read the z words. Trace each one. Then write it two times.

zone

zigzag

zipper

zombie

Morning Jumpstarts: Reading, Grade 2 © 2013 Scholastic Teaching Resources

📖 Ready, Set, READ!

Read. Then answer the questions.

The Magic Shell

Pink shells, white shells,
Shells of gray and blue.
Smooth shells, crinkled shells,
Shells both old and new.
Striped shells, spotted shells
Tumbled by the tide.
But my shell has magic—
The ocean sings inside!

The Power of a Smile

A smile is such a happy thing.
It crinkles up your face.
And when it's gone you never know
Its secret hiding place.
I think it's just a wonder
To see what smiles can do.
I smile at you, you smile at me,
And so one smile makes two!

1. Both poems use the word *crinkle*. Which word means the same?

　○ A. tickle　　　○ B. sparkle　　　○ C. crease

2. Why does the poet say "my shell has magic"?

_____

3. What does the poet say is the smile's power?

_____

Sentence Mender

Rewrite the sentence to make it correct.

they be the betterest team of all.

_____

⊙ BrainTeaser ⊙

How many different words can you spell with letters from the word **mousetrap**? Every word must have at least three letters. List them here.

_____

_____

82

Morning Jumpstarts: Reading, Grade 2 © 2013 Scholastic Teaching Resources

Name _____ Date _____

Morning Jumpstarts: Reading, Grade 2 © 2013 Scholastic Teaching Resources

WORD of the Day

urban: related to a city or busy town

Use the word **urban** to describe a city activity to try.

_____

_____

FUN Phonics

Draw lines to match the *contraction* with two words that mean the same. The first one is done for you.

you'll •	• they will
I'll •	• it will
they'll •	• I will
it'll •	• I have
I've •	• we have
you've •	• you will
we've •	• let us
let's •	• you have

> **Contract** means *to get smaller.*

Handwriting Helper

Read the *weather* words. Trace each one. Then write it two times.

weather

storm

lightning

thunder

Ready, Set, READ!

Read. Then answer the questions.

Dear Mr. Jakes,

　　My name is Darci Owens. I am eight years old. I live next door to you. I'm writing to ask you a favor.

　　I like your dog Major. It's fun to watch him play. I don't mind it when he barks. But my sister Nola is afraid of dogs. She's only four, so she doesn't go outside by herself, even in our yard. But she won't even come with me if Major is outside. His loud bark scares her.

　　Do you think we could make an after-school time when you keep Major inside? That way Nola and I can play in our yard. Maybe you could keep Major inside between 3:30 and 5:00 PM? Or maybe you could show Nola how to make friends with Major? She might be less afraid if you are there.

　　Thank you for thinking about this favor. You can call us at 555-5555.

Your neighbor,
Darci

1. Why does Darci write to Mr. Jakes?
   - ○ A. to ask a favor
   - ○ B. to complain
   - ○ C. to offer help

2. How are Darci and Nola alike?

   _____

   _____

   _____

   How are they different?

   _____

   _____

   _____

Sentence Mender

Rewrite the sentence to make it correct.

Our clas has twenty-for childs.

_____

☺ BrainTeaser ☺

What does each saying mean? Write the number on the line.

1. It's time to **throw in the towel**.　　_____ live on less money

2. Oh, **go fly a kite**.　　_____ go away

3. **Tighten your belt**.　　_____ Try something new.

4. Why don't you **get your feet wet**?　　_____ Someone is ready to quit.

Morning Jumpstarts: Reading, Grade 2 © 2013 Scholastic Teaching Resources

Name _____ Date _____

WORD of the Day

rotate: to turn around in a circle, like a wheel

Use the word **rotate** to write about a tool that helps you turn something.

_____

_____

FUN Phonics

Complete the chart. Add **-s**, **-ed**, and **-ing** to each base word.

Base Word	-s	-ed	-ing
park			
test			
round			
order			
paint			

Handwriting Helper

Read the *time* words. Trace each one. Then write it.

yesterday

today

tomorrow

future

📖 Ready, Set, READ!

Read. Then answer the questions.

Mr. William Frisbie had a pie company in Connecticut. Students at a nearby school loved his fresh pies. They paid for each pie, plus five cents. They would get the nickel back if they gave back the pie tin. But some kids never gave the tins back. They turned them into toys instead. They liked to toss the tins into the air and try to catch them. They yelled "Frisbie" to warn friends if the tin was coming at them.

Many years later, a toy company decided to make a pie-tin toss toy out of plastic. The plastic toy flew farther and was easier to aim than an old pie tin. It could be made in colors. It would never rust or have sharp parts. They named the plastic toy a "Frisbee."

Did the pie company inspire the toy? Maybe, but it's hard to know for sure. Both names sound alike but have different spellings.

1. Why did some kids keep used pie tins?

_____

_____

_____

_____

_____

_____

2. What does the word *inspire* mean?
   - ○ A. warn someone
   - ○ B. fly far
   - ○ C. bring about

Sentence Mender

Rewrite the sentence to make it correct.

There house is maid of logs.

_____

⤜ BrainTeaser ⤛

What does each saying mean? Write the number on the line.

1. She is **all thumbs**.　　　　　_____ Stay cheerful.

2. Who will **break the ice**?　　　_____ Do the whole job.

3. Don't **cut corners**.　　　　　_____ Someone is clumsy.

4. **Keep your chin up**.　　　　　_____ Someone must go first.

Morning Jumpstarts: Reading, Grade 2 © 2013 Scholastic Teaching Resources

Name _____ Date _____

WORD
of the Day

fragment: a small piece or broken-off part

Use the word **fragment** to write what scientists can tell from a piece of bone.

_____

_____

FUN Phonics

Complete the chart. Add **-s**, **-ed**, and **-ing** to each base word.
Drop silent *e* when needed.

Base Word	-s	-ed	-ing
raise			
smile			
describe			
erase			
wiggle			

Handwriting Helper

Read the *writing* words. Trace each one. Then write it two times.

sentence

capital

comma

period

Ready, Set, READ!

Read. Then answer the questions.

The Boy Who Cried "Wolf!"

A young boy cared for a flock of sheep. He found his days dull, so he made a plan for some fun. He ran into the village and waved his arms, crying, "Wolf! Wolf!" The villagers raced to help, only to find the boy laughing. "Go tend to your flock!" they scolded.

The boy was so pleased with his trick that he repeated it the next day. Once again, the villagers were fooled. "You're a liar!" they scolded.

The boy went back to his flock and saw a hungry wolf sneaking toward them. The sheep began to cry in fear. The boy raced to the village faster than ever. He cried loudly, "Wolf! Wolf! Really!" This time the villagers paid no attention. They thought he was just playing his same old trick. So the wolf filled his belly and the boy cried bitter tears.

Moral: *No one believes a liar, even when he tells the truth.*

1. Why did the boy call for help the first two times?

_____

_____

_____

_____

_____

2. What is the lesson of this tale?
   ○ A. Never shout.
   ○ B. Be kind to animals.
   ○ C. Don't lie.

Sentence Mender

Rewrite the sentence to make it correct.

Did him borrow abbys book

_____

⌕ BrainTeaser ⌕

What does each saying mean? Write the number on the line.

1. **Sleep on it** first.   _____ scolded

2. gave **a piece of my mind**   _____ energy

3. so much **get-up-and-go**   _____ wants to back out

4. always **gets cold feet**   _____ think about it for a while

Morning Jumpstarts: Reading, Grade 2 © 2013 Scholastic Teaching Resources

Name _____ Date _____

WORD of the Day

joyous: filled with joy; very happy; merry

Use the word **joyous** to write how to mark a happy event.

FUN Phonics

Fill in the chart. Add **-er** and **-est** to each base word. Think about spelling changes you may need to make. The first row is done for you.

Base Word	-er	-est
fast	faster	fastest
high		
small		
safe		
silly		

RULES
- Drop silent *e*
- Change *y* to *i*

Handwriting Helper

Read the words that tell about how much. Trace each word. Then write it two times.

almost

nearly

close to

around

Ready, Set, READ!

Read. Then answer the questions.

Islands come in all shapes and sizes. Some are flat and dry, and others are hilly and green. Some islands have cities on them. Others have plants and animals, but no people at all.

An island can be near the land or far out to sea. It can be in a river or a lake. The thing that all islands have is water all around them.

If you fly over an island and look down, how will it look? You might think it looks like a floating bath toy. You might wonder how the island got there.

A toy boat is already a boat before you sail it in your tub. But islands build up over time. They are made of rock and sand. Some form when waves drop sand near the coast. Rocky islands can form when lava from a volcano cools off. Islands can also form when water splits one piece of land away from the rest.

1. Why does the writer compare islands to bath toys?

_____

_____

_____

_____

2. Which is not how an island forms?
   ○ A. It falls from the sky.
   ○ B. Sand builds up.
   ○ C. Water splits it off.

Sentence Mender

Rewrite the sentence to make it correct.

Kevin comed to see me game.

_____

☉ BrainTeaser ☉

Use the clues to complete words that start with *sha*.

1. Large ocean fish   S H A ____ ____

2. Blocked from sun   S H A ____ ____

3. Broken-down house   S H A ____ ____

4. Like a very furry dog   S H A ____ ____ ____

5. Soap to wash hair   S H A ____ ____

90

Name _____ Date _____

WORD
of the Day

proof: facts that show something is true

Use the word **proof** to tell a way to show your age.

_____

_____

FUN Phonics

Read the poem. Count how many syllables are in each word. Then write each word in the chart where it belongs.

> I wonder if the bumblebees
>   That buzz around our pepper trees
>   Ever sneeze?

1 syllable	2 syllables	3 syllables

Handwriting Helper

Read the *direction* words. Trace each one. Then write it.

horizontal

vertical

forward

backward

Ready, Set, READ!

Read. Then answer the questions.

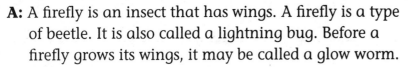

Q: What is a firefly?

A: A firefly is an insect that has wings. A firefly is a type of beetle. It is also called a lightning bug. Before a firefly grows its wings, it may be called a glow worm.

Q: What makes a firefly glow?

A: A firefly has special organs in its tail to make light. The light it makes stays cold. The glowing tail gives off no heat.

Q: Why does a firefly glow in the first place?

A: Fireflies glow to find mates. Males and females send light signals to each other. The flashes also warn away hunters that might eat the firefly. The light tells the hunters that the firefly will taste bad.

Q: Where do fireflies live?

A: Most fireflies live in grassy areas near water. You see them most often on warm, muggy nights.

1. What do **Q** and **A** stand for?

   _____

   _____

2. Which is *not* a name for a firefly?
   - A. glow worm
   - B. lightning bug
   - C. stink bug

3. *True* or *false*: Fireflies feel hot to touch.

   _____

Sentence Mender

Rewrite the sentence to make it correct.

The car Because we ran out a gas

_____

BrainTeaser

Use the clues to complete words that start with *chi*.

1. Young boy or girl   C H I ____ ____

2. Bird sound   C H I ____ ____

3. Most important person   C H I ____ ____

4. A little bit cold   C H I ____ ____ ____

5. Lays eggs   C H I ____ ____ ____ ____

Morning Jumpstarts: Reading, Grade 2 © 2013 Scholastic Teaching Resources

Name _____ Date _____

WORD of the Day

history: everything that happened in the past

What time in the past would you like to visit? Use the word **history** to write about it.

_____

_____

FUN Phonics

A *prefix* is a word part you add at the beginning of a word.
It changes the meaning.
The prefix *re-* means **again**. The prefix *un-* means **not**.
Write a *re-* or *un-* word to fit each phrase.
The first one is done for you.

1. tie again _retie_____   4. not safe _____

2. not happy _____   5. use again _____

3. fill again _____   6. not able _____

Handwriting Helper

Read the *shape* words. Trace each one. Then write it.

circle

square

triangle

rectangle

📖 Ready, Set, READ!

Read. Then answer the questions.

Sally Gooding   *Traditional Folk Song*

I had a piece of pie and I had a dish of pudding.
I gave them all away just to see Sally Gooding!
I don't miss the pie and I don't miss the pudding.
All I really miss is my little Sally Gooding.

I love potato pie and I love apple pudding.
But best of all I love my pretty Sally Gooding.
I left behind the pie and I left behind the pudding
To cross the big river to see Sally Gooding.

Sally is my rosebud, Sally is my daisy.
If she won't see me I might go crazy!
Sweet as wild honey and pink as a berry.
Dear Sally Gooding is the gal I want to marry!

1. What makes verse 3 different from the first two verses?

_____

_____

_____

_____

_____

2. Which feeling best fits the person singing to Sally?
   ○ A. anger
   ○ B. fear
   ○ C. love

3. Read the song with rhythm. Try to make up a tune for it!

Sentence Mender

Rewrite the sentence to make it correct.

Us picked a apple from it's tree.

_____

⦿ BrainTeaser ⦿

Unscramble the words so that all rhyme.

1. rdoo _____   4. arro _____

2. orpu _____   5. esrot _____

3. ehrco _____   6. lrofo _____

94

Morning Jumpstarts: Reading, Grade 2 © 2013 Scholastic Teaching Resources

Name _____ Date _____

<table>
<tr><td>**WORD of the Day**</td><td>**careless**: not paying attention; without care

Use the word **careless** to write a warning about what could happen at the beach.</td></tr>
</table>

_____

_____

FUN Phonics

The prefixes **dis-** and **non-** mean **the opposite of.**
Write a **dis-** or **non-** word to fit each phrase. The first one is done for you.

1. the opposite of agree	4. the opposite of living
disagree	
2. the opposite of fiction	5. the opposite of please
3. the opposite of order	6. the opposite of sticky

Handwriting Helper

Read the boys' names. Trace each one. Then write it two times.

Itamar

Roberto

Wayne

Xavier

Ready, Set, READ!

Read. Then answer the questions.

Cleo and Tim love biking with their parents. Mom and Dad have adult bikes. Cleo and Tim have kid bikes that connect to the back of each adult bike. Both riders hold and pedal, but the adults always steer.

Yesterday the family began a six-day trip. They plan to ride mostly through farmland. They'll stop at farm stands or diners for food. They'll camp out at night.

Mom and Tim led the way. They began early, before it got too hot. Dad and Cleo rode behind, but would lead later. Each pair talked as they rode.

Their first big stop was around noon. They rode into a park that had a lake and picnic tables. It felt great to rest, eat, and cool off in the water. Cleo checked the maps as Dad stretched out. Tim drew in his sketch book as Mom used her smart phone to check the weather.

1. How long will the trip last?

   _____

   _____

2. What time of year do you think this is?
   - ○ A. spring
   - ○ B. summer
   - ○ C. fall

Sentence Mender

Rewrite the sentence to make it correct.

I got the book Trumpet of the Swan on sail

_____

☺ Brain Teaser ☺

A *noun* names a person, a place, a thing, or an idea.

Write two more examples in the chart for each kind of noun. Examples are done for you.

Person nouns	Place nouns	Thing nouns	Idea nouns
principal	kitchen	bookshelf	kindness

Morning Jumpstarts: Reading, Grade 2 © 2013 Scholastic Teaching Resources

Name _____ Date _____

WORD of the Day

dissolve: to mix completely into water

Use the word **dissolve** to write about something a cook mixes into hot water.

_____

_____

FUN Phonics

A *suffix* is a word part you add at the end of a word. It changes the meaning. Write the word with its suffix to fit each phrase.

–ful = **full of** *fearful*	–ly = **like** *ghostly*	–ly = **in some way** *oddly*
1. full of hope _____	3. like a friend _____	5. in a brave way _____
2. full of joy _____	4. like a mother _____	6. in a proud way _____

Handwriting Helper

Read the *girls'* names. Trace each one. Then write it two times.

Bonnie

Maria

Nancy

Ursula

 # Ready, Set, READ!

Read. Then answer the questions.

Maine Fog   *A Tall Tale*

They say that fog in Maine is as thick as logs. Maine fog is tough, and it won't burn off so fast. Maine fog is so thick you can drive nails into it to hang your boots up. You could bet your boat on that!

Now Old Willy works a fishing boat, but he knows to stay on land when that Maine fog rolls in. He does his chores on foggy days. Yesterday was a chore day. Willy set out to nail new shingles onto his cabin roof. He began just after breakfast and didn't come back down until suppertime. "Sarah," Willy told his wife, "we sure got us a long house! My shingling took me this whole day."

Now Sarah knew they lived in a small cabin. She'd been caring for it for years! So out she went for a look. And what did she see? Willy had shingled past the edge of the roof and right onto the fog!

1. What does "bet your boat on that" mean?

   ○ A. It would be safe to bet your boat because you wouldn't lose.

   ○ B. It's a good time to trade in your boat when it's foggy.

   ○ C. A boat is a smart thing to bet because it's worth a lot.

2. Explain the joke at the end of the story.

   _____

   _____

   _____

Sentence Mender

Rewrite the sentence to make it correct.

Wood the cat be all bedder by next weak?

_____

☺ BrainTeaser ☺

What starts with *T*, ends with *T*, and is full of *T*?

Solve each clue. Then copy each letter into its numbered box to find the answer to the riddle.

• Tiny round veggie ___ ___ ___
　　　　　　　　　4　 2　 3

• Small child ___ ___ ___
　　　　　　　6　 5　 1

1	2	3	4	5	6

Morning Jumpstarts: Reading, Grade 2 © 2013 Scholastic Teaching Resources

Name _____   Date _____

WORD of the Day

example: a model of a rule or pattern; one of a group to help you understand it

Use the word **example** to describe something that is cold.

_____

_____

FUN Phonics

A *suffix* is a word part you add at the end of a word. It changes the meaning. Write the word with its suffix to fit each phrase.

–ness = **state of being** *soft**ness***	–less = **without** *use**less***
1. state of being dark _____	3. without care _____
2. state of being shy _____	4. without end _____

Handwriting Helper

Read the *city* names. Trace each one. Then write it two times.

Denver

Orlando

Chicago

Boston

Ready, Set, READ!

Read. Then answer the questions.

This is my review of *Finding Nemo*. It's a cartoon movie. My mom thought I would like it. So we made popcorn and watched it together on TV.

Nemo is a young fish who lives in the ocean. His dad tries to teach him to be careful, but Nemo loves to explore. He gets caught by a diver one day and doesn't come back. His dad goes wild with worry, so he sets out to find Nemo. That's what the title means.

The dad fish must swim far from home. He isn't brave, but he makes himself go. He faces danger from sharks and other creatures. He even has to find Nemo in a big city. But I won't spoil the ending.

Mom was right. This was a really good movie. It was funny, scary, and pretty to watch. It was odd that the dad was more scared than Nemo. My mom says that good parents always worry about their kids.

1. Which best tells how the writer feels about the movie?
   - O A. She had a hard time following the story.
   - O B. She didn't want to watch, but her mom made her.
   - O C. She liked the movie and was glad she saw it.

2. How does she not spoil the ending?

   _____

   _____

   _____

   _____

Sentence Mender

Rewrite the sentence to make it correct.

My fathr don't speak english very well.

_____

꩜ BrainTeaser ꩜

Hink Pinks are word pairs that rhyme to answer riddles. Here's a Hink Pink: ～～～➤

What is a large kitten?
fat cat

Solve these Hink Pinks. Fill in the missing word for each.

1. What is travel by boat? **ship** _____

2. What is a simple choo-choo? **plain** _____

3. What is a contest with fire? **game** _____

Morning Jumpstarts: Reading, Grade 2 © 2013 Scholastic Teaching Resources

Name _____ Date _____

WORD of the Day

puzzling: confusing; unclear; like a mystery

Use the word **puzzling** to write about a confusing event.

_____

_____

FUN Phonics

A *compound word* is made of two smaller words put together. Write the compound word that names each picture.

1. _____ 2. _____ 3. _____

  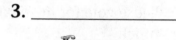

4. _____ 5. _____ 6. _____

Handwriting Helper

Read the language names. Trace each one. Then write it two times.

English _____

Spanish _____

Korean _____

Russian _____

Morning Jumpstarts: Reading, Grade 2 © 2013 Scholastic Teaching Resources

📖 Ready, Set, READ!

Read. Then answer the questions.

Hello, friends. I am here to ask you to vote for me. I want to be our new class president. I hope to make our school an even better place. Kids at our school are full of good ideas. If I get elected, I will try to get some kid-friendly ideas put into place. I hope you will help that happen.

My best idea is for us kids to have gym time each day. Now we have gym just twice a week. This is too little. We all need time to run, jump, play, and stay fit. I will talk with the principal. Maybe we can think of ways to fix this. Maybe big kids could play with little kids. Teams could maybe have more players. We could have shorter gym times, but have them five times a week instead of two.

Please vote for me next Tuesday. Thank you very much.

1. What change does the speaker want?

_____

_____

_____

_____

2. What reasons support this change?

_____

_____

_____

_____

Sentence Mender

Rewrite the sentence to make it correct.

Ones upon a time they're was an dragon.

_____

⊚ BrainTeaser ⊚

Fill in each blank with a word that makes sense.

1. I would like _____ for breakfast.

2. The dog hid its bone in the _____.

3. Juan likes to paint pictures of _____.

4. Keesha found a _____ during her walk.

5. Did you see that _____ butterfly?

Morning Jumpstarts: Reading, Grade 2 © 2013 Scholastic Teaching Resources

Name _____ Date _____

Morning Jumpstarts: Reading, Grade 2 © 2013 Scholastic Teaching Resources

WORD of the Day

perform: to do a task; to give a public show

Use the word **perform** to explain teaching a pet a trick.

_____

_____

FUN Phonics

A *compound word* is made of two smaller words put together.
Write the compound word that names each picture.

1. _____   2. _____   3. _____

4. _____   5. _____   6. _____

Handwriting Helper

Read the story character names. Trace each one. Then write it two times.

Anansi _____

Eeyore _____

Ramona _____

Horton _____

📖 Ready, Set, READ!

Read. Then answer the questions.

Some ideas come along when you don't expect them. This happened to a man named George in 1948. He went hiking in the woods with his dog. When George and his dog got home, they were covered with sticky burrs (seed pods). George had burrs stuck to his pants. The dog had them stuck to its fur.

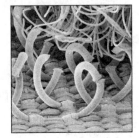
Look for tiny hooks and loops.

George wanted to know what made all those burrs stick so well. So he used his microscope (MIKE-ruh-skope) to look up close at some burrs. He saw that each burr had many tiny hooks that could "grab" his pants or the dog's fur. Those tiny hooks held on very tightly!

The hooks gave George an idea. He invented a new product to hold two things together tightly. One part of it had lots of tiny hooks. The other part had lots of soft little loops. The hooks and loops stuck together!

1. George hiked to
   ○ A. think about inventions.
   ○ B. get exercise and enjoy nature.
   ○ C. get to another city.

2. Which is George's invention?
   ○ A. duct tape
   ○ B. the zipper
   ○ C. Velcro

Sentence Mender

Rewrite the sentence to make it correct.

Its almost time to leaf for the buss.

_____

⑨ BrainTeaser ⑥

Fill in each blank with a word that makes sense.

1. Megan forgot to _____ her boots.

2. The frog jumped into a _____.

3. Willy climbed up a tall _____.

4. Don't raise your voice in the _____.

5. Would you like a cup of _____?

Morning Jumpstarts: Reading, Grade 2 © 2013 Scholastic Teaching Resources

Name _____   Date _____

WORD of the Day

habitat: the natural home of an animal, plant, or other living thing

Use the word **habitat** to write about where a beaver lives.

_____

_____

FUN Phonics

A *synonym* is a word that means the same or almost the same as another word. Draw lines to match each word on the left with its synonym on the right. The first one is done for you.

find •	• auto
car •	• right
yell •	• wealthy
gift •	• crave
correct •	• present
want •	• locate
rich •	• shout

Handwriting Helper

Read the questions. Trace each one. Then write it.

Where is Zambia?

When is Valentine's Day?

Morning Jumpstarts: Reading, Grade 2 © 2013 Scholastic Teaching Resources

Ready, Set, READ!

Read. Then answer the questions.

The First Tears   *An Inuit Folktale*

Long ago, Man went hunting by the sea for seal. He hoped to catch one to share with Woman and Child, for they were all hungry. But the seals were too fast. They slid into the water before Man could get near. Then Man saw one lone seal far from the water.

He crept quietly toward the seal. But as he got nearer, the seal wiggled away and slipped into the sea. Man felt an odd feeling. Water fell from his eyes. He touched and tasted the drops, which were as salty as the sea. Choking sounds got stuck in his throat.

Child heard the sounds. Child and Woman ran to find out what was wrong. They saw the water flowing from Man's eyes. Man told them that he did not catch a seal. He felt ashamed. Soon water began to fall from the eyes of Woman and Child as well. And this is how people first learned to cry.

1. Why did Man feel ashamed?
   - ○ A. He was crying.
   - ○ B. He failed to catch a seal.
   - ○ C. He was far from his family.

2. How can you tell this is a folktale?
   - ○ A. It tells how something began.
   - ○ B. It has only three people in it.
   - ○ C. It can't be true.

Sentence Mender

Rewrite the sentence to make it correct.

We new dr Chen was from china.

_____

☺ BrainTeaser ☺

Think about how the first two words go together. Then copy the word that fits the other word in the same way.

> EXAMPLE
> **Pen** is to **write** as **ax** is to __chop__.
> sharp   chop   hammer

1. **Snow** is to **flake** as **rain** is to _____.
   wet   water   drop

2. **Bee** is to **hive** as **bird** is to _____.
   wing   nest   air

3. **Hot** is to **fire** as **cold** is to _____.
   ice   winter   warm

Morning Jumpstarts: Reading, Grade 2 © 2013 Scholastic Teaching Resources

Name _____ Date _____

WORD of the Day

incorrect: wrong; not true

Use the word **incorrect** to write one way your teacher shows a wrong answer on a test.

_____

_____

FUN Phonics

Antonyms are words that mean the opposite.
Draw lines to match each word on the left with its antonym on the right. The first one is done for you.

answer •	• sunset
dawn •	• good
finish •	• rough
evil •	• polite
plump •	• thin
rude •	• question
gentle •	• begin

Handwriting Helper

Read the questions. Trace each one. Then write it.

How much is the apple?

Which is your cubby?

Morning Jumpstarts: Reading, Grade 2 © 2013 Scholastic Teaching Resources

📖 Ready, Set, READ!

Read. Then answer the questions.

Do you like food? Do you have a good eye for shape and color? If so, there is a job you might not know of. It's the job of a food stylist. It's like being a hair stylist, but with food instead of hair. A stylist knows how to make something look as good as it can. Food stylists help to make our mouths water!

I bet you have seen ads for foods that look so tasty you could eat the page! Part of this is the work of the food stylist. That person makes the food look too yummy to miss! The stylist uses tricks to make food look great.

Some foods in an ad may be unsafe to eat—even if they look amazing! One trick is to use shaving cream instead of whipped cream! Of course, that would be awful to eat. But real whipped cream can't stay puffy under the hot lights of a photo studio. Shaving cream doesn't mind the heat!

1. What does a food stylist do?

_____

_____

_____

2. Why switch shaving cream for whipped cream?

_____

_____

_____

Sentence Mender

Rewrite the sentence to make it correct.

The cartoon chipmunks are name Alvin Simon Theodore.

_____

🌀 BrainTeaser 🌀

Think about how the first two words go together. Then copy the word that fits the other word in the same way.

> EXAMPLE
> **Pen** is to **write** as **ax** is to chop .
> sharp   chop   hammer

1. **Branch** is to **tree** as **toe** is to _____.
   finger   foot   leaf

2. **Bed** is to **sleep** as **ladder** is to _____.
   wood   pillow   climb

3. **Nice** is to **mean** as **grumpy** is to _____.
   cheery   old   wicked

Morning Jumpstarts: Reading, Grade 2 © 2013 Scholastic Teaching Resources

Answers

Jumpstart 1
Word of the Day: Sample response—Mittens always come in a **pair**.
Fun Phonics: 1. b **2.** h **3.** d **4.** f **5.** v **6.** m
Handwriting Helper: Check children's work for accuracy and legibility.
Ready, Set, Read! 1. C **2.** The blue moon has to be the second full moon in a month.
Sentence Mender: Sample response—Dad made a shopping list.
Brainteaser: (Top to bottom) black, yellow, purple, green; blue

Jumpstart 2
Word of the Day: Sample response—I do puzzles to keep **busy** on a rainy day.
Fun Phonics: 1. s **2.** k **3.** b **4.** t **5.** f **6.** d
Handwriting Helper: Check children's work for accuracy and legibility.
Ready, Set, Read! 1. C **2.** They use sound words to add fun and meaning to the song.
Sentence Mender: Jason read the whole book.
Brainteaser: (Top to bottom) four, nine, seven, zero; five

Jumpstart 3
Word of the Day: Sample response—I don't like it when my friends **boast**.
Fun Phonics: 1. b **2.** g **3.** v **4.** l **5.** p **6.** r
Handwriting Helper: Check children's work for accuracy and legibility.
Ready, Set, Read! 1. crown, root **2.** Both have roots you can't see.
Sentence Mender: Did you write this poem?
Brainteaser: (Top to bottom) May, June, April, March; year

Jumpstart 4
Word of the Day: Sample response—I would see a **dune** at the beach.
Fun Phonics: 1. B **2.** M **3.** B **4.** E **5.** E **6.** M
Handwriting Helper: Check children's work for accuracy and legibility.
Ready, Set, Read! 1. C **2.** Petting Zoo **3.** Craft City
Sentence Mender: My bedtime is eight o'clock.
Brainteaser: Answers will vary; samples include: sleep, shiny, sling

Jumpstart 5
Word of the Day: Sample response—I feel **glum** when I am sick.
Fun Phonics: 1. m **2.** r **3.** n **4.** m **5.** n **6.** m **7.** n **8.** r **9.** r
Handwriting Helper: Check children's work for accuracy and legibility.
Ready, Set, Read! 1. She's going to her new school by herself for the first time. **2.** He used a sharp, loud warning.
Sentence Mender: Please don't say those mean words.
Brainteaser: Answers will vary; samples include: clerk, clank, click, skunk

Jumpstart 6
Word of the Day: Sample response—I am trying to **grasp** how a radio works.
Fun Phonics: 1. e **2.** a **3.** e **4.** a **5.** i **6.** u
Handwriting Helper: Check children's work for accuracy and legibility.
Ready, Set, Read! 1. B **2.** C
Sentence Mender: My sister Katy didn't shut the door.
Brainteaser: Answers will vary; check children's word lists.

Jumpstart 7
Word of the Day: Sample response—My **chore** at home is to set the table.
Fun Phonics: (Left to right) sample answers: -*ack* words—track, smack, pack; -*ap* words—clap, snap, trap, gap; -*ank* words—thank, bank, yank, frank; -*ash* words—cash, dash, bash, gash; -*at* words—flat, rat, brat, pat
Handwriting Helper: Check children's work for accuracy and legibility.
Ready, Set, Read! 1. B **2.** Sample answer: A gazebo is a small house that has screens instead of windows.
Sentence Mender: Mike gave us a ride in his new car.
Brainteaser: 1. arm **2.** pat or apt **3.** ring **4.** spot or tops

Jumpstart 8
Word of the Day: Sample response—It is **polite** to say thank you when someone helps you at a store.
Fun Phonics: (Left to right) sample answers: -*ell* words—spell, smell, tell; -*est* words—rest, best, test, guest; -*eck* words—deck, peck, check, wreck; -*ent* words—rent, sent, gent, bent; -*ess* words—mess, chess, bless, guess
Handwriting Helper: Check children's work for accuracy and legibility.
Ready, Set, Read! 1. 6 **2.** C
Sentence Mender: Your class was going to the park.
Brainteaser: 1. blow **2.** lump **3.** west or wets **4.** seat or teas or eats

Jumpstart 9
Word of the Day: Sample response—I love to **glide** across a shiny wooden floor.
Fun Phonics: (Left to right) sample answers: -*ick* words—trick, stick, pick; -*ill* words—will, pill, hill, still; -*ing* words—sing, wing, bring, thing; -*ink* words—pink, sink, wink, think; -*itch* words—stitch, witch, pitch, hitch
Handwriting Helper: Check children's work for accuracy and legibility.
Ready, Set, Read! 1. B **2.** To tie a loop at the top of the pinecone for hanging **3.** To spread the peanut butter on the cone
Sentence Mender: The teacher said to shut our eyes.
Brainteaser: 1. big **2.** hen's **3.** flat

Jumpstart 10
Word of the Day: Sample response—Honking horns **distract** me when I'm reading.
Fun Phonics: (Left to right) sample answers: -*ock* words—smock, clock, flock; -*op* words—top, mop, stop, flop; -*ob* words—rob, gob, slob, blob; -*og* words—hog, frog, bog, clog; -*ox* words—fox, box, lox, mailbox
Handwriting Helper: Check children's work for accuracy and legibility.
Ready, Set, Read! 1. Sample response: Kermit was born in 1955, but did not become famous for many years. **2.** 21
Sentence Mender: Yesterday we had pizza for lunch.
Brainteaser: Answers may vary; one solution: bat, bag, big

Jumpstart 11
Word of the Day: Sample response—I like to hide in a **hollow** tree.
Fun Phonics: (Left to right) sample answers: -*uck* words—cluck, muck, tuck; -*ug* words—hug, bug, rug, snug; -*ump* words—bump, clump, hump, dump; -*unk* words—skunk, bunk, trunk, junk; -*ush* words—brush, rush, crush, blush
Handwriting Helper: Check children's work for accuracy and legibility.
Ready, Set, Read! 1. They wanted a child so much, they didn't care. **2.** B
Sentence Mender: The wind blew down a tree near my house.
Brainteaser: Answers may vary; one solution: tick, lick, lock, tock

Jumpstart 12
Word of the Day: Sample response—I **claim** that my dog is part human.
Fun Phonics: 1. track **2.** drill **3.** nest **4.** truck **5.** frog **6.** witch
Handwriting Helper: Check children's work for accuracy and legibility.
Ready, Set, Read! 1. B **2.** C
Sentence Mender: Can you reach up to the highest shelf?
Brainteaser:

```
Q U V U U H P O C Z N
R B T O O K A Q R E
U B W C I T E C S U I
R A E B U A M T D N G
A N S T R E E T S N H
L V I L L A G E K E B
Q Q C L F H M S A R O
R R I T L K Q T T T R
C I T I Z E N A E O M
D Y Y T O W N T T R A
```

Jumpstart 13

Word of the Day: Sample response—I would most like to see a whale **calf**.
Fun Phonics: Rhymes in 2, 3, 7, 8
Handwriting Helper: Check children's work for accuracy and legibility.
Ready, Set, Read! 1. Ogden Nash **2.** Answers may vary but each has four lines that rhyme. **3.** I know what loving means, and I know –est means the most, like in tallest.
Sentence Mender: Let's meet after school to trade baseball cards.
Brainteaser:

G	E	M	P	E	A	C	G	O	I
P	R	J	E	A	H	A	S	L	G
T	O	Y	B	C	C	O	A	L	R
C	C	P	B	S	B	D	N	L	A
V	K	Z	L	J	W	F	D	V	V
U	P	Y	E	P	S	T	O	N	E
M	I	N	E	R	A	L	S	R	L
G	Y	M	R	A	C	K	H	O	O
Q	J	B	S	H	O	N	E	C	G

Jumpstart 14

Word of the Day: Sample response—There is **plenty** of space to play soccer in the park.
Fun Phonics: 1. can; possible answer: take **2.** pan; possible answer: tail **3.** had; possible answer: gray **4.** gal; possible answer: late
Handwriting Helper: Check children's work for accuracy and legibility.
Ready, Set, Read! 1. B **2.** She planned to cover the junk under dirty laundry.
Sentence Mender: Our new cows and horses eat fresh hay.
Brainteaser: Answers will vary; check children's lists.

Jumpstart 15

Word of the Day: Sample response—I am happy to **arrive** at the ice-cream stand.
Fun Phonics: 1. sell; possible answer: meal **2.** bend; possible answer: tree **3.** set; possible answer: need **4.** tent; possible answer: peel
Handwriting Helper: Check children's work for accuracy and legibility.
Ready, Set, Read! 1. Maybe Jada was trying to sharpen the pencil. **2.** C
Sentence Mender: Mr. Gold drives a school bus.
Brainteaser: Answers will vary; check children's lists.

Jumpstart 16

Word of the Day: Sample response—A cactus grows in the **desert**.
Fun Phonics: 1. lick; possible answer: rice **2.** bread; possible answer: tide **3.** kit; possible answer: night **4.** tray; possible answer: dry
Handwriting Helper: Check children's work for accuracy and legibility.
Ready, Set, Read! 1. B **2.** They longed to fly so much.
Sentence Mender: They went to the San Diego Zoo.
Brainteaser: 1. rainbow **2.** starfish 3. snowbank

Jumpstart 17

Word of the Day: Sample response—It's hard to be **honest** if you think you might get in trouble.
Fun Phonics: 1. box; possible answer: moat **2.** spot; possible answer: woke **3.** cow; possible answer: low **4.** bun; possible answer: cone
Handwriting Helper: Check children's work for accuracy and legibility.
Ready, Set, Read! 1. C **2.** Sample answer: He makes a joke about the hawk.
Sentence Mender: We will land in one hour in Portland, Maine.
Brainteaser: The word is *tardy*.

C	H	A	R	T
P	A	S	T	A
R	I	V	E	R
T	H	I	R	D
W	I	N	D	Y

Jumpstart 18

Word of the Day: Sample response—I **suppose** there will be a cake at the party.
Fun Phonics: 1. tube; possible answer: lube **2.** blue; possible answer: true **3.** mute; possible answer: cute **4.** chew; possible answer: threw
Handwriting Helper: Check children's work for accuracy and legibility.
Ready, Set, Read! 1. C **2.** 7:00
Sentence Mender: I was born on Monday, June 9, right?
Brainteaser: The color is *brown*.

E	L	B	O	W
H	O	R	N	S
P	H	O	T	O
T	O	W	E	R
V	E	N	U	S

Jumpstart 19

Word of the Day: Sample response—It's hard to see when you drive in a **blizzard**.
Fun Phonics: 1. suit **2.** two **3.** roof **4.** soup
Handwriting Helper: Check children's work for accuracy and legibility.
Ready, Set, Read! 1. The child's father taught him/her. **2.** The star in the middle of the flag looks like the hole in the bread where the egg goes.
Sentence Mender: We march in a parade on New Year's Day.
Brainteaser: 1. dress **2.** socks **3.** scarf **4.** shirt **5.** jacket **6.** jeans

Jumpstart 20

Word of the Day: Sample response—I like to watch stars **sparkle** in the sky at night.
Fun Phonics: (Left to right) long *a*—flake, tray; long *e*—heat, free; long *i*—child, pie, sigh; long *o*—foam, both; long *u*—cute, fruit, tune. Check the words children add for accuracy.
Handwriting Helper: Check children's work for accuracy and legibility.
Ready, Set, Read! 1. C **2.** There were so many steps in making them.
Sentence Mender: Can't you see the kitten on the roof?
Brainteaser: 1. whale **2.** lion **3.** tiger **4.** panda **5.** rabbit **6.** monkey

Jumpstart 21

Word of the Day: Sample response—I **predict** I will live on a farm when I grow up.
Fun Phonics: $\overline{oo}$—fool, room, spoon; $\breve{oo}$—cook, foot, hood
Handwriting Helper: Check children's work for accuracy and legibility.
Ready, Set, Read! 1. B **2.** I think Nick will go on the spaceship to Mars.
Sentence Mender: I didn't see the dog's tail under my chair.
Brainteaser: 1. Open your eyes. **2.** She must wash up. **3.** Do you like my cat?

Jumpstart 22

Word of the Day: Sample response—A busy street is a **danger** for a small child.
Fun Phonics: 1. car, shore **2.** thorns, sharp **3.** corn, farm **4.** sport, hard **5.** horse, smart
Handwriting Helper: Check children's work for accuracy and legibility.
Ready, Set, Read! 1. C **2.** B
Sentence Mender: She will come stay with us for two weeks.
Brainteaser: 2. wishes **3.** messes **5.** spoons **6.** shapes

Jumpstart 23

Word of the Day: Sample response—A **sturdy** ladder makes climbing safer and easier.
Fun Phonics: h*er*d—fern, germ, serve; b*ir*d—first, girl, stir; n*ur*se—burn, fur, hurt
Handwriting Helper: Check children's work for accuracy and legibility.
Ready, Set, Read! 1. C **2.** A
Sentence Mender: Let's play checkers. I will take red.
Brainteaser: 2. man **3.** hero **4.** tooth **5.** child **6.** fox

Jumpstart 24

Word of the Day: Sample response—I think my heart would **flutter** if I saw a movie star.
Fun Phonics: 1. i **2.** e **3.** e **4.** i **5.** i **6.** e
Handwriting Helper: Check children's work for accuracy and legibility.
Ready, Set, Read! 1. B **2.** He wanted to make the neighborhood look better.
Sentence Mender: His mom leaves for work at six o'clock in the morning.
Brainteaser: 1. toss **2.** finish **3.** loud

Morning Jumpstarts: Reading, Grade 2 © 2012 Scholastic Teaching Resources

Jumpstart 25

Word of the Day: Sample response—I hear bees buzzing around the flowers in the **meadow**.
Fun Phonics: 1. alarm **2.** again **3.** adult **4.** agree. **5.** awake **6.** asleep **7.** ago **8.** about **9.** apart
Handwriting Helper: Check children's work for accuracy and legibility.
Ready, Set, Read! 1. A sound sleeper is hard to wake up. **2.** C
Sentence Mender: Randy's new house has two floors.
Brainteaser: Answers will vary; samples: **1.** rush **2.** fix **3.** shy **4.** tired

Jumpstart 26

Word of the Day: Sample response—I'm **eager** to get home to ride my bike.
Fun Phonics: 1. H **2.** S **3.** H **4.** S **5.** H **6.** S **7.** H **8.** H **9.** S
Handwriting Helper: Check children's work for accuracy and legibility.
Ready, Set, Read! 1. C **2.** A
Sentence Mender: Maria asked if she could use Dad's tool kit.
Brainteaser: Answers will vary; samples: **1.** pal **2.** heal **3.** pick **4.** easy

Jumpstart 27

Word of the Day: Sample response—Can you **explain** why the sky is blue?
Fun Phonics: 1. H **2.** S **3.** S **4.** H **5.** S **6.** S **7.** S **8.** H **9.** S
Handwriting Helper: Check children's work for accuracy and legibility.
Ready, Set, Read! 1. B **2.** She wanted to leave them for the fairy babies.
Sentence Mender: Jack and Jill carry a pail of water.
Brainteaser: 1. asleep **2.** float **3.** smile **4.** summer

Jumpstart 28

Word of the Day: Sample response—My **dwelling** would be 100 feet tall and have hundreds of rooms!
Fun Phonics: Answers may vary; samples: **1.** broom, groom **2.** fresh **3.** crisp **4.** brook, crook **5.** drift **6.** grapes, drapes **7.** crust, trust **8.** crank, drank, Frank, prank **9.** frump, grump
Handwriting Helper: Check children's work for accuracy and legibility.
Ready, Set, Read! 1. B **2.** C
Sentence Mender: My favorite numbers are four, seven, eleven, and sixteen.
Brainteaser: Answers will vary; samples, left to right: booming, silent; silky, rocky

Jumpstart 29

Word of the Day: Sample response—A blue whale is a **mammoth** sea creature.
Fun Phonics: Answers may vary; samples: **1.** place **2.** flea **3.** glove **4.** blade **5.** sleep **6.** click **7.** bloom **8.** glue **9.** slush
Handwriting Helper: Check children's work for accuracy and legibility.
Ready, Set, Read! 1. A **2.** Traci was going to read a biography of him.
Sentence Mender: The winners were Tom, Billy, Jake, and Lynda.
Brainteaser: Answers will vary; samples, left to right: wreck, fix; speedy, sluggish

Jumpstart 30

Word of the Day: Sample response—I like to **relax** by drawing cartoons.
Fun Phonics: 1. small **2.** swim **3.** sleeve **4.** star **5.** scare **6.** spoil
Handwriting Helper: Check children's work for accuracy and legibility.
Ready, Set, Read! 1. They learned that they could write a sports story if they had one. **2.** Possible answer: It's way too short!
Sentence Mender: Our teacher is reading Mr. Peabody's Apples to us.
Brainteaser: Answers may vary; samples:

	B	L	S	T
Toys	ball	Legos	scooter	train
Foods	bacon	lettuce	soup	tacos
Animals	beaver	lizard	snake	turtle

Jumpstart 31

Word of the Day: Sample response—Last night, I saw the sun set in the **distance**.
Fun Phonics: 1. desk **2.** gift **3.** stamp **4.** cold **5.** quilt **6.** hand
Handwriting Helper: Check children's work for accuracy and legibility.
Ready, Set, Read! 1. It explains how bluebirds got their color. **2.** B
Sentence Mender: We don't have any shoe polish.
Brainteaser: Sentences will vary; sample: **S**am's **s**ister **S**uzy **s**weetly **s**ang **s**even **s**illy **s**ummer **s**ongs.

Jumpstart 32

Word of the Day: Sample response—I get **homesick** for my puppy.
Fun Phonics: 1. dri**nk** **2.** te**nt** **3.** bi**rd** **4.** sha**rk** **5.** che**st** **6.** wa**sp**
Handwriting Helper: Check children's work for accuracy and legibility.
Ready, Set, Read! 1. C **2.** It smells the plant's sweet smell.
Sentence Mender: Jack might be late tomorrow.
Brainteaser: Sentences will vary; sample: **T**ell **T**ommy **T**inker **t**o **t**aste **t**en **t**omatoes.

Jumpstart 33

Word of the Day: Sample response—The children **cluster** at the window to watch the lightning.
Fun Phonics: 1. chicken **2.** shade **3.** phone **4.** thirty **5.** where **6.** show
Handwriting Helper: Check children's work for accuracy and legibility.
Ready, Set, Read! 1. C **2.** Ron thinks Ivy is wasting her time.
Sentence Mender: Dad missed the train by a whole hour!
Brainteaser: Sentences will vary; sample: **L**azy **m**onkeys **n**ibble **o**ld **p**otatoes.

Jumpstart 34

Word of the Day: Sample response—The **aircraft** I'd like to fly in is a helicopter because you can see down.
Fun Phonics: 1. cough **2.** graph **3.** peach **4.** sing **5.** tooth **6.** goldfish
Handwriting Helper: Check children's work for accuracy and legibility.
Ready, Set, Read! 1. It is caused by cold food touching the roof of your mouth. **2.** C
Sentence Mender: Mr. Davis is the new principal of my school.
Brainteaser: 1. over **2.** with **3.** because **4.** water

Jumpstart 35

Word of the Day: Sample response—Lost pets get food and water in an animal **shelter**.
Fun Phonics: 1. ring **2.** finger **3.** long **4.** hanger **5.** swing **6.** stinger
Handwriting Helper: Check children's work for accuracy and legibility.
Ready, Set, Read! 1. A **2.** Sample answer: The cat eats the pancake.
Sentence Mender: She had a bad sore throat for two days.
Brainteaser: Answers will vary; samples: -ack—track, rack; -ame—game, flame; -ell—bell, well

Jumpstart 36

Word of the Day: Sample response—I stood quietly to **observe** a mother bird feeding her chick.
Fun Phonics: 1. boil, enjoy, point **2.** royal, coin, voice **3.** Joyce, Troy, Leroy **4.** shout, howl, cloud **5.** meow, crown, pout, flower **6.** allow, ouch, loud
Handwriting Helper: Check children's work for accuracy and legibility.
Ready, Set, Read! 1. B **2.** C
Sentence Mender: I finished my lunch so now I'll play soccer.
Brainteaser: 1. backpack **2.** handstand **3.** barnyard **4.** downtown

Jumpstart 37

Word of the Day: Sample response—Stuart Little is a **gritty** little mouse.
Fun Phonics: (Top to bottom) can't/cannot; didn't/did not; isn't/is not; doesn't/does not; haven't/have not; wouldn't/would not; aren't/are not
Handwriting Helper: Check children's work for accuracy and legibility.
Ready, Set, Read! 1. C **2.** The poet hears the sound of the sea inside it. **3.** One person's smile makes another person smile, too.
Sentence Mender: They are the best team of all.
Brainteaser: Answers will vary; check children's word lists.

Jumpstart 38

Word of the Day: Sample response—My aunt grows her own veggies in an **urban** garden.
Fun Phonics: (Top to bottom) I'll/I will; they'll/they will; it'll/it will; I've/I have; you've/you have; we've/we have; let's/let us
Handwriting Helper: Check children's work for accuracy and legibility.
Ready, Set, Read! 1. A **2.** Both girls are sisters; Darci likes dogs but Nola is afraid of them.
Sentence Mender: Our class has twenty-four children.
Brainteaser: 3, 2, 4, 1

Jumpstart 39

Word of the Day: Sample response—Use a wrench to **rotate** a tight nut.
Fun Phonics:

Base Word	-s	-ed	-ing
park	parks	parked	parking
test	tests	tested	testing
round	rounds	rounded	rounding
order	orders	ordered	ordering
paint	paints	painted	painting

Handwriting Helper: Check children's work for accuracy and legibility.
Ready, Set, Read! 1. They used them as flying toys. **2.** C
Sentence Mender: Their house is made of logs.
Brainteaser: 4, 3, 1, 2

Jumpstart 40

Word of the Day: Sample response—A scientist can tell from a bone **fragment** what animal it came from.
Fun Phonics:

Base Word	-s	-ed	-ing
raise	raises	raised	raising
smile	smiles	smiled	smiling
describe	describes	described	describing
erase	erases	erased	erasing
wiggle	wiggles	wiggled	wiggling

Handwriting Helper: Check children's work for accuracy and legibility.
Ready, Set, Read! 1. He wanted to have some fun and trick the villagers. **2.** C
Sentence Mender: Did he borrow Abby's book?
Brainteaser: 2, 3, 4, 1

Jumpstart 41

Word of the Day: Sample response—Music and dancing help make a wedding more **joyous**.
Fun Phonics:

Base Word	-er	-est
fast	faster	fastest
high	higher	highest
small	smaller	smallest
safe	safer	safest
silly	sillier	silliest

Handwriting Helper: Check children's work for accuracy and legibility.
Ready, Set, Read! 1. Both have water all around them. **2.** A
Sentence Mender: Kevin came to see my game.
Brainteaser: 1. shark **2.** shady **3.** shack **4.** shaggy **5.** shampoo

Jumpstart 42

Word of the Day: Sample response—Mom has a paper from the hospital where I was born to show **proof** of my age.
Fun Phonics: 1 syllable—I, if, the, that, buzz, our, trees, sneeze; 2 syllables—wonder, around, pepper, ever; 3 syllables—bumblebees
Handwriting Helper: Check children's work for accuracy and legibility.
Ready, Set, Read! 1. Question, Answer **2.** C **3.** False
Sentence Mender: The car stopped because we ran out of gas.
Brainteaser: 1. child **2.** chirp **3.** chief **4.** chilly **5.** chicken

Jumpstart 43

Word of the Day: Sample response—I'd like to go back in **history** to when there were dinosaurs.
Fun Phonics: 2. unhappy **3.** refill **4.** unsafe **5.** reuse **6.** unable
Handwriting Helper: Check children's work for accuracy and legibility.
Ready, Set, Read! 1. Verse 3 uses two different rhymes. **2.** C
Sentence Mender: We picked an apple from its tree.
Brainteaser: 1. door **2.** pour **3.** chore **4.** roar **5.** store **6.** floor

Jumpstart 44

Word of the Day: Sample response—If you're **careless** on a beach, you may step on a sharp shell.
Fun Phonics: 2. nonfiction **3.** disorder **4.** nonliving **5.** displease **6.** nonsticky
Handwriting Helper: Check children's work for accuracy and legibility.
Ready, Set, Read! 1. six days **2.** B
Sentence Mender: I got the book <u>Trumpet of the Swan</u> on sale.
Brainteaser: Answers will vary; check children's lists.

Jumpstart 45

Word of the Day: Sample response—You **dissolve** powder in hot water to make Jello.
Fun Phonics: 1. hopeful **2.** joyful **3.** friendly **4.** motherly **5.** bravely **6.** proudly
Handwriting Helper: Check children's work for accuracy and legibility.
Ready, Set, Read! 1. A **2.** Willy got tricked by the thick fog.
Sentence Mender: Would the cat be all better by next week?
Brainteaser: pea, tot; teapot

Jumpstart 46

Word of the Day: Sample response—Snow is an **example** of something that is cold.
Fun Phonics: 1. darkness **2.** shyness **3.** careless **4.** endless
Handwriting Helper: Check children's work for accuracy and legibility
Ready, Set, Read! 1. C **2.** She doesn't tell exactly if, when, or how the father finds Nemo.
Sentence Mender: My father doesn't speak English very well.
Brainteaser: 1. trip **2.** train **3.** flame

Jumpstart 47

Word of the Day: Sample response—It's **puzzling** to me that a tornado can lift up a car.
Fun Phonics: 1. backpack **2.** cupcake **3.** beehive **4.** baseball **5.** cowboy **6.** bathtub
Handwriting Helper: Check children's work for accuracy and legibility.
Ready, Set, Read! 1. The speaker wants more gym time. **2** The speaker thinks kids have too little exercise time now.
Sentence Mender: Once upon a time there was a dragon.
Brainteaser: Answers will vary; check children's sentences for reasonableness.

Jumpstart 48

Word of the Day: Sample response—I taught my dog to **perform** tricks as I beat a drum.
Fun Phonics: 1. fireplace **2.** mailbox **3.** football **4.** sailboat **5.** rainbow **6.** snowman
Handwriting Helper: Check children's work for accuracy and legibility.
Ready, Set, Read! 1. B **2.** C
Sentence Mender: It's almost time to leave for the bus.
Brainteaser: Answers will vary; check children's sentences for reasonableness.

Jumpstart 49

Word of the Day: Sample response—A beaver's **habitat** is a dam built in a forest stream.
Fun Phonics: (Top to bottom) car/auto; yell/shout; gift/present; correct/right; want/crave; rich/wealthy
Handwriting Helper: Check children's work for accuracy and legibility.
Ready, Set, Read! 1. B **2.** A
Sentence Mender: We knew Dr. Chen was from China.
Brainteaser: 1. drop **2.** nest **3.** ice

Jumpstart 50

Word of the Day: Sample response—My teacher marks **incorrect** answers with a red circle.
Fun Phonics: (Top to bottom) dawn/sunset; finish/begin; evil/good; plump/thin; rude/polite; gentle/rough
Handwriting Helper: Check children's work for accuracy and legibility.
Ready, Set, Read! 1. The food stylist makes food look as good as it can.
2. Shaving cream will keep its shape.
Sentence Mender: The cartoon chipmunks are named Alvin, Simon, and Theodore.
Brainteaser: 1. foot **2.** climb **3.** cheery

Morning Jumpstarts: Reading, Grade 2 © 2013 Scholastic Teaching Resources